New Day

Edited by **Gordon Giles** May–August 2024

 Ministries

15 The Chambers, Vineyard,
Abingdon OX14 3FE
+44 (0)1865 319700 | brf.org.uk

Bible Reading Fellowship is a charity (233280)
and company limited by guarantee (301324),
registered in England and Wales

ISBN 978 1 80039 259 5
All rights reserved

This edition © Bible Reading Fellowship 2024
Cover photo by saturnus99/pexels.com

Distributed in Australia by:
MediaCom Education Inc, PO Box 610, Unley, SA 5061
Tel: 1 800 811 311 | admin@mediacom.org.au

Distributed in New Zealand by:
Scripture Union Wholesale, PO Box 760, Wellington 6140
Tel: 04 385 0421 | suwholesale@clear.net.nz

Acknowledgements

A catalogue record for this book is available from the British Library

Printed by Gutenberg Press, Tarxien, Malta

Suggestions for using *New Daylight*

Find a regular time and place, if possible, where you can read and pray undisturbed. Before you begin, take time to be still and perhaps use the prayer of BRF Ministries on page 6. Then read the Bible passage slowly (try reading it aloud if you find it over-familiar), followed by the comment. You can also use *New Daylight* for group study and discussion, if you prefer.

The prayer or point for reflection can be a starting point for your own meditation and prayer. Many people like to keep a journal to record their thoughts about a Bible passage and items for prayer. In *New Daylight* we also note the Sundays and some special festivals from the church calendar, to keep in step with the Christian year.

New Daylight and the Bible

New Daylight contributors use a range of Bible versions, and you will find a list of the versions used opposite. You are welcome to use your own preferred version alongside the passage printed in the notes. This can be particularly helpful if the Bible text has been abridged.

New Daylight affirms that the whole of the Bible is God's revelation to us, and we should read, reflect on and learn from every part of both Old and New Testaments. Usually the printed comment presents a straightforward 'thought for the day', but sometimes it may also raise questions rather than simply providing answers, as we wrestle with some of the more difficult passages of scripture.

New Daylight is also available in a compact size edition. Visit your local Christian bookshop or BRF's online shop **brfonline.org.uk**. To obtain an audio version for the blind or partially sighted, contact Torch Trust for the Blind, Torch House, Torch Way, Northampton Road, Market Harborough LE16 9HL; +44 (0)1858 438260; **info@torchtrust.org**.

Comment on *New Daylight*

To send feedback, please email **enquiries@brf.org.uk**, phone **+44 (0)1865 319700** or write to the address shown opposite.

Writers in this issue

Louise Davis lives in Leicester where she spends most of her time gardening, both at home and on her allotment. When she is not up to her elbows in dirt, she works with children and families at Leicester Cathedral.

Martin Leckebusch worked in IT for 37 years before retiring to spend more time writing. He lives in Gloucester, is an elder at a Baptist church and is the author of over 500 published hymn texts.

Michael Mitton is a freelance writer, speaker, spiritual director and canon emeritus of Derby Cathedral. He has been a parish priest, the director of Anglican Renewal Ministries, the deputy director of the Acorn Christian Healing Foundation and the fresh expressions officer for the diocese of Derby. He is author of *Restoring the Woven Cord* (BRF, 2019), among other books.

John Ryeland is ordained in the Church of England and was the director of The Christian Healing Mission for over 25 years. He is the author of several books, including *Encountering the God who Heals* (Malcolm Down Publishing, 2017).

Harry Smart is an Anglican priest and has spent most of his ministry as a mental health chaplain. He now has a special responsibility for staff wellbeing and patients with mental health problems in general health care in Hull.

Naomi Starkey is a priest in the Church in Wales, based in a group of North Anglesey churches and also working more widely as a pioneer evangelist.

David Walker is bishop of Manchester. He is the author of *God's Belongers* (BRF, 2017), professor of Anglican studies at Bishop Grosseteste University, a regular presenter of BBC Radio 4's *Thought for the Day* and a member of the Third Order of the Society of St Francis.

Jane Walters is the author of *Too Soon* (SPCK, 2018) and chair of the Association of Christian Writers. She runs a writing group in mid-Norfolk and creative writing retreats further afield. **janewyattwalters.com**

Catherine Williams is an Anglican priest working as a spiritual director and freelance writer. She contributes regularly to a variety of devotional, biblical and preaching resources. Catherine is also the lead voice on the Church of England's *Daily Prayer* and *Time to Pray* apps.

Gordon Giles writes…

Easter was a month ago, relatively early this year. Perhaps you know that Easter is calculated as being the first Sunday after the first full moon after the vernal equinox (20 March). Easter always falls in spring, therefore, and can be as early as 22 March (if 21 March is a Saturday and has a full moon). That last happened in 1818. In 2000 we saw the latest possible Easter, 23 April. This year's date for Easter – 31 March – is not so rare; it was the same day in 2013.

Every Easter is a pausing point on the spiritual highway, which parks us on a new Golgotha hill, with the same view changed by seasons and circumstances. The perspective is altered. For we and everything and everyone else have changed, sometimes imperceptibly, sometimes radically. If we have lost someone, the idea of death and resurrection will strike us in ways that may be challenging or comforting, or both. For others it may just be 'another Easter', a couple of bank holidays with ancient Christian heritage, blessed only with hints of longer days and spring flowers.

Meanwhile every year there are some who are truly affected, deeply, perhaps for the first time, by the very presence of the risen Lord, deep in their hearts, breathing Holy Spirit down necks that have become unstiffened, at last. Whatever Easter has been for you, whatever it has done and is doing to you this year, *notice*, give thanks and do not let it ebb away.

For after Easter day we speak of Eastertide. Tides come in waves, literally. Every year these tides – Christmas, Epiphany, Passion, Easter and Ascension – ebb and flow. Now that Eastertide has washed us in its baptismal waters again, where will it bear us as it goes out? We cannot know, we cannot tell. Yet if the psychologists are right, our ability to imagine the future is buried in our capacity to remember the past. For while we can remember, we can imagine too, and imagination is one of the greatest Easter presents. For buried in memory are the seeds of imagination, which rise up and become a flowering of hope.

This edition we welcome two new authors, Martin Leckebusch and Catherine Williams, both of whom will help us use our imaginations in new Eastertide ways as we journey into spring and summer.

The prayer of BRF Ministries

Faithful God,
thank you for growing BRF
from small beginnings
into the worldwide family of BRF Ministries.
We rejoice as young and old
discover you through your word
and grow daily in faith and love.
Keep us humble in your service,
ambitious for your glory
and open to new opportunities.
For your name's sake,
Amen.

'It is such a joy to be part of this amazing project'

As part of our Living Faith ministry, we're raising funds to give away copies of Bible reading notes and other resources to those who aren't able to access them any other way, working with food banks and chaplaincy services, in prisons, hospitals and care homes.

'This very generous gift will be hugely appreciated, and truly bless each recipient… Bless you for your kindness.'

'We would like to send our enormous thanks to all involved. Your generosity will have a significant impact and will help us to continue to provide support to local people in crisis, and for this we cannot thank you enough.'

If you've enjoyed and benefited from our resources, would you consider paying it forward to enable others to do so too?

Make a gift at **brf.org.uk/donate**

Silence

Early in Jesus' ministry, after a long and hectic day of teaching and healing, his disciples wake up the next morning and discover him gone. Eventually, he is tracked down to a quiet and lonely spot, where he has gone to be close to God. That pattern of balancing silence with the demands of a busy life has always meant a great deal to me. When I became a Franciscan tertiary in 1991, I pledged to follow Jesus after the example of St Francis of Assisi, a man who likewise combined a busy life of service and travel with extended periods of retreat and silence. In my prayer life, I have come to value both silent times at home with God and the use of silence in church services. Indeed, there is something that touches me deeply in the companionable silence of a crowd of worshippers.

Such silence, freely chosen, can be deeply restorative. But both my life experiences and my reflections on the Bible have taught me to see silence as a much broader and more nuanced concept. Sometimes we have to hold our tongues in order to allow others space to speak. Beyond that, we may need to discipline ourselves to listen to what they are saying, rather than be preparing our own next comments. Nor is silence always positive. Remaining silent in the face of injustice and deliberately silencing the voices of victims are often powerful instruments of oppression and abuse.

Scripture speaks too of God's silence, a silence that Jesus experiences on the cross. Earlier, the psalmists plead with God to break his silence, beseeching Israel's Lord to intervene, so that the righteous can receive vindication and the wicked be punished. Our faith needs a basis for understanding why such divine silence is not a sign of God's absence or lack of care for his people.

The passages for these ten days take us through a wide range of how silence is depicted in the scriptures. Many are comforting; one or two may be, for some readers, disturbing. All are, I believe, valuable in helping us understand the role that silence plays in our faith. That in turn will help us know when and how best to embrace silence as part of our own spiritual practice, as well as when to speak.

DAVID WALKER

God made known in silence

'Go out and stand on the mountain before the Lord, for the Lord is about to pass by.' Now there was a great wind, so strong that it was splitting mountains and breaking rocks in pieces before the Lord, but the Lord was not in the wind, and after the wind an earthquake, but the Lord was not in the earthquake, and after the earthquake a fire, but the Lord was not in the fire, and after the fire a sound of sheer silence. When Elijah heard it, he wrapped his face in his mantle and went out and stood at the entrance of the cave. Then there came a voice to him that said, 'What are you doing here, Elijah?'

In olden times, the presence of a divine being was often signified by powerful physical phenomena. Think of the Norse god Thor, throwing thunderbolts, or the attribution of storms to warring factions among the Roman or Greek deities. Israel's own God has earlier been revealed to Moses in a burning bush. At this stage in Elijah's life, he is beginning to despair that he is the only one left who has not succumbed to the worship of false gods. He needs a powerful god, one who can uphold him in the face of overwhelming odds. So, when God tells him to stand on the mountain, he is expecting something along the lines of the wind, earthquake and fire that ensue. What surprises Elijah is that God himself is in none of these. Instead, 'The Lord' is present in 'a sound of sheer silence' (v. 12). Only after this does God speak.

Finding God in silence stands at the core of the spiritual lives of many Christians. Not least when, like Elijah, we fear being overwhelmed by the noisiness, busyness, aggression and opposition of the world around us. In silence we sense the God who loves us and delights in us and who has much more to offer us than mere sound and fury.

Lord God, you made yourself known to Elijah in silence;
help me to know your presence today. Whenever my life feels full of noise
and distraction, be my quiet, still centre. Amen.

DAVID WALKER

A time to keep silent

'Look, my eye has seen all this; my ear has heard and understood it. What you know, I also know; I am not inferior to you. But I would speak to the Almighty, and I desire to argue my case with God. As for you, you whitewash with lies; all of you are worthless physicians. If you would only keep silent, that would be your wisdom!… Let me have silence, and I will speak, and let come on me what may.'

Job begins the book that bears his name wealthy and well blessed. Yet in a short season of disasters, he has seen everything dear to him snatched away. Three friends, traditionally referred to as 'Job's comforters', have come to speak with him. They offer all manner of conventional explanations; perhaps he has some secret sin for which his suffering is the price exacted. But to Job their words ring hollow. What he needs is not worldly wisdom but to be allowed to plead his case before God. That granted, he stands ready to bear whatever consequences may befall him.

Over my years as both priest and bishop, I have sat with many sufferers. Friends and family, like Job's companions, often try to articulate reasons and explanations for what has gone so dreadfully wrong. Somebody, usually some outside individual or organisation, must be to blame, and be held to account. Yet what the sufferer often most needs is to express their emotions, to know they have been heard, not to have their feelings twisted either to rationalisation or revenge. Sometimes my role has been to sit in silence while they pour out their hearts. On occasion it has been to be the proxy for the God whom they wish to berate over what has befallen them. It is only, as the unfolding story bears out, when Job has had his say with God, that healing and restitution can follow.

Heavenly Father, help me this day to listen well, to know when to keep silence, so that others might speak, and to refrain from offering words when words are not needed, so that those who truly need to speak can be heard and their voices carry both to earth and to heaven. Amen.

DAVID WALKER

God will break silence to vindicate the innocent

Do not be silent, O God of my praise. For wicked and deceitful mouths are opened against me, speaking against me with lying tongues… But you, O Lord my Lord, act on my behalf for your name's sake; because your steadfast love is good, deliver me… With my mouth I will give great thanks to the Lord; I will praise him in the midst of the throng. For he stands at the right hand of the needy, to save them from those who would condemn them to death.

The Psalms express a wonderful wealth of human experience. Today, we hear the voice of those pleading with God to speak in their defence. Surely the Lord will not remain silent while the wicked utter words of deceit, nor stand idly by while they condemn the innocent and return evil for good?

Yet this psalm is not merely a cry of complaint. It ends, as many others do, on an upbeat note. God may be silent for now, but that silence will not last forever. In an image that evokes comparisons with a legal advocate standing by a defendant, God will stand at the right hand of the needy and ensure their acquittal.

I have been active on social media for over a decade. As someone in the public eye, I have got used to what are often referred to as 'trolls'. These people, almost always anonymous, expend their energies on criticism, accusation and abuse. The more unfair the critique, the more tempting it is to respond. Yet to do so is to fall into a trap. Every response merely magnifies their audience. Every counter argument leads to more, and more vicious, abuse. I have learned to ignore their remarks and, if they persist, to use the 'mute' button to stop me seeing what they write.

Social media merely magnifies what we experience elsewhere. Sometimes we need to ignore criticism, to remain silent. We need to remember that God, who knows the secrets of all hearts, is our advocate and the only judge whose verdict finally matters.

Heavenly Father, help me to live this day in the knowledge that you,
who knows my innermost thoughts, are my sure defender.
Where words will not help my cause, grant me the gift of silence. Amen.

DAVID WALKER

Silent for our sakes

He was oppressed, and he was afflicted, yet he did not open his mouth; like a lamb that is led to the slaughter and like a sheep that before its shearers is silent, so he did not open his mouth. By a perversion of justice he was taken away. Who could have imagined his future? For he was cut off from the land of the living, stricken for the transgression of my people. They made his grave with the wicked and his tomb with the rich, although he had done no violence, and there was no deceit in his mouth.

This excerpt from Isaiah, from a passage often entitled 'The suffering servant', is one of the most often quoted of the Hebrew prophetic writings. Since the days of the early church, Christians have seen it as a prophecy about the Messiah; the one who will come to bear the sins of the world. It forms a central text for many Advent and Christmas services. It resonates both with John the Baptist's entitling of Jesus as the lamb of God and with the gospel descriptions of him refusing to answer questions at his trial. As he hangs on the cross, Jesus will be taunted by the crowd: if he really is God's Son, why does he not command an army of angels to rescue him? Their taunts have been referred to as Christ's last temptation.

Yet to have spoken such words of power would have been a denial of his destiny. Instead, he has to trust in his heavenly Father, whose own silence he feels deeply at that moment. His call is to endure, and in due time to commend his spirit into God's hands. This silence has not been to defend himself, nor to avoid further challenge. It is not for his own sake; it is for the sake of those for whom he has come to accomplish his mission. He is silent so that we might have a voice before heaven.

Lord Jesus Christ, for my sake you suffered in silence before your torturers, even to the very point of death, that I might have an advocate in heaven. Help me this day to be grateful for your love, which, through pain and persecution, held you to your purpose. Amen.

DAVID WALKER

Resting in calm and quiet

O Lord, my heart is not lifted up; my eyes are not raised too high; I do not occupy myself with things too great and too marvellous for me. But I have calmed and quieted my soul, like a weaned child with its mother; my soul is like the weaned child that is with me. O Israel, hope in the Lord from this time on and forevermore.

This is one of the shortest psalms in the Bible but also one of the most beautiful. As a father to two children, that image of the weaned child, no longer crying out with a hunger beyond its infant understanding, but rather quiet and at peace in the presence of its mother, is wonderfully resonant for me. Just as the child can now enjoy the security and safety that mother provides, so I can rest in God's presence.

It's a psalm I need to remember when I find myself confronted with complexities that lie beyond my ability to disentangle. It is there for me when disputes, especially disputes between Christians, and even members of the same church, prove beyond my capacity to resolve. It reassures me that the world is not a problem I have been appointed to solve. Rather, my first duty is to be present with God, without anxiety or anger. Quietly, by God's calm presence, I will be shown what, if anything, it falls to me to do in a given situation. Beyond that, just as for the child playing in their mother's presence, wider and greater matters are for others to manage.

Nor is this anything particular to my present calling as bishop of a diocese. Whoever we are, and whatever tasks God has or has not entrusted to us, I believe we can and should find that place where we play at peace in his presence. Not least when we go to bed at night, we can ask God to calm our wandering thoughts and to reassure us that everything lies ultimately in his control. While we sleep or play, like the mother in the psalm, he both continues his work and watches over us.

Lord God, help me to rest in your presence, especially when the work of the day is done. Grant me quiet and peace in which to replenish my energies and to know that your loving eyes are ever watching over me. Amen.

DAVID WALKER

A shameful silence

Tamar took the cakes she had made and brought them into the chamber to Amnon her brother. But when she brought them near him to eat, he took hold of her and said to her, 'Come, lie with me, my sister.' She answered him, 'No, my brother, do not force me; for such a thing is not done in Israel; do not do anything so vile!'… But he would not listen to her, and being stronger than she, he forced her and lay with her… Her brother Absalom said to her, 'Has Amnon your brother been with you? Be quiet for now, my sister; he is your brother; do not take this to heart.' So Tamar remained, a desolate woman, in her brother Absalom's house. When King David heard of all these things, he became very angry, but he would not punish his son Amnon, because he loved him, for he was his firstborn.

I find the incestuous rape of Tamar one of the most disturbing stories of the scriptures. Amnon's behaviour may not be condoned, but his status as David's firstborn is deemed more important than justice for his abused sister. Tamar's story resonates when abuses by celebrities, politicians or church leaders, including both financial and sexual offences, are brushed under the carpet. Three millennia on from the assault on Tamar, there are still leaders whose importance is reckoned, even by Christians, to sanction a shroud of silence being placed over their crimes. Tragically, when one victim or survivor breaks cover, it often becomes clear that what had been presented as a single fall from grace was in fact a repeated pattern of abusive behaviour, extending over many years.

But even if it were a single occurrence, such abuse of power should never be weighed against other considerations. It is, as Tamar says, in the one moment she is allowed a voice, 'a thing not done in Israel'. The challenge of this text is that, unlike King David, we should have courage to let the cry of the survivor be heard.

Lord God, comforter of the abused, grant us courage
to never condemn victims to silence in the name of some higher purpose,
but to hear and to amplify the voices of the survivors,
that justice might be done, on earth as in heaven. Amen.

DAVID WALKER

Interrupting the silence

As they were leaving Jericho, a large crowd followed him. There were two blind men sitting by the roadside. When they heard that Jesus was passing by, they shouted, 'Lord, have mercy on us, Son of David!' The crowd sternly ordered them to be quiet, but they shouted even more loudly, 'Have mercy on us, Lord, Son of David!' Jesus stood still and called them, saying, 'What do you want me to do for you?' They said to him, 'Lord, let our eyes be opened.' Moved with compassion, Jesus touched their eyes. Immediately they regained their sight and followed him.

In days before voice amplification, we can easily imagine the scene. An outdoor setting, a throng of people so eagerly wanting to catch the wisdom falling from the lips of Jesus that they are largely silent in his presence. Suddenly, their ability to hear his words is disrupted by two noisy beggars. Even worse, the more they try to shut them up, the louder they cry.

I've stood among crowds myself, trying to concentrate on what the speaker is saying, resentful of hecklers who have come intent on disrupting proceedings. And I have sat in theatres, frustrated by distracting chatter between fellow attendees. But these beggars seek neither to distract nor disrupt. Like the crowd, they want to engage with Jesus. Yet these two have a more particular ask than simply to enjoy the words of a celebrity teacher. They have heard of his power to heal, and they want it exercised on their behalf. Nor are they finished with Jesus once their request has been answered; rather, they immediately follow him. They have gained more than just physical sight.

This passage challenges me because, in protecting the silence of my surroundings, I do not always make the effort to distinguish what is justifiable interruption. Jesus makes that distinction, recognising the impact he can have on their lives as outweighing a few moments of disruption to the listening crowd.

Lord Jesus, open my ears, not only to your words, but to the voices of those I hear cry to you in need. May I never be a hindrance in their reaching out to you, but always an encourager, that your name may be glorified. Amen.

DAVID WALKER

A contrast in silence

What use is an idol once its maker has shaped it – a cast image, a teacher of lies? For its maker trusts in what has been made, though the product is only an idol that cannot speak! Alas for you who say to the wood, 'Wake up!' to silent stone, 'Rouse yourself!' Can it teach? See, it is gold and silver plated, and there is no breath in it at all. But the Lord is in his holy temple; let all the earth keep silence before him!

Again and again, Israel's prophets draw a sharp contrast between the idols that the people were constantly tempted to fashion and worship, and the one true God, the maker of all. No matter how long and loud their makers implore these gods of wood or metal to speak, they remain the mere mute objects they have always been. Shaping them into the semblance of beasts or human beings cannot give them breath, nor provide them with words or wisdom. Noisy worshippers will not conjure words from the wordless. Conversely, God himself, present in his temple, commands not words but quiet from his own creation. If anyone is to break this silence, it will be he himself, the Lord.

Today, we may not fashion our idols from wood or metal; instead we have found subtler media. Some of us create idols of celebrities or sports stars, politicians or church leaders. We hang on their words, assuming they have expertise far beyond their professional status or learning. Others among us place our trust in some TV channel, social media group or website. No wonder some so-called 'influencers' can command enormous sums in return for promoting products. I suspect we may soon discover how to make idols out of artificial intelligence. We implore these to teach us, with all the same vigour that the people of old did their gold and wooden gods. Yet in doing so, we distract ourselves, just as much as our forebears ever did, from attending to the wisdom that God seeks to offer.

---

*Heavenly Father, you alone are God, you alone speak with full authority.
Help me this day not to place my trust in earthly things,
but to listen in silence for your voice of wisdom and to boldly follow
wherever you may lead me. Amen.*

DAVID WALKER

The silenced season

When they had come together, they asked him, 'Lord, is this the time when you will restore the kingdom to Israel?' He replied, 'It is not for you to know the times or periods that the Father has set by his own authority. But you will receive power when the Holy Spirit has come upon you, and you will be my witnesses in Jerusalem, in all Judea and Samaria, and to the ends of the earth.' When he had said this, as they were watching, he was lifted up, and a cloud took him out of their sight.

I am largely supportive of how the Church of England celebrates the various seasons of the church year. My one exception is the decision to make the focus for the period after today, Ascension Day, until Pentecost, a week on Sunday, the coming of the Holy Spirit. Perhaps the fact that I was born on Ascension Day gives me a particular concern for what it implies. I do not want its message silenced by too rapid a move to what comes next.

For the first disciples there was no such immediate jump. The departure of Jesus, with no Holy Spirit yet given to empower them, leaves them in an in-between time, a time when God himself is silent. And yet they are not without a purpose. Luke, at the end of his gospel, describes how during these ten days they were constantly in the temple, worshipping God.

I live a pretty busy life. I need to remember that there are times when what is asked of me is not to be working at the next priority, nor catching up on a backlog of unanswered emails, but to pause. For what may be several days, or even longer, my call may be to devote myself simply to being present before God, alongside others, in worship. This season of Ascensiontide, as we might call it, could be just that, if only it had not been silenced.

Lord Jesus Christ, you gave your disciples ten days to abide in worship before you anointed them with your Holy Spirit. Grant us, likewise, space to dwell in your presence, united with our sisters and brothers, before you call us on to such further endeavours as you have prepared for us. Amen.

DAVID WALKER

When silence must be broken

My anguish, my anguish! I writhe in pain! Oh, the walls of my heart! My heart is beating wildly; I cannot keep silent, for I hear the sound of the trumpet, the alarm of war. Disaster overtakes disaster, the whole land is laid waste. Suddenly my tents are destroyed, my curtains in a moment. How long must I see the standard and hear the sound of the trumpet? 'For my people are foolish, they do not know me; they are stupid children; they have no understanding. They are skilled in doing evil but do not know how to do good.'

This passage is written in part from the perspective of the prophet, looking at the destruction imminently facing Israel, and in part from that of God. The frustration in God's words, as his chosen people reject both God and good is palpable. It is a frustration the prophet shares. It drives him to speak out, whether or not his words will be heeded. To call someone a 'Jeremiah' most commonly carries the implication that they are unduly negative, or causing alarm where alarm is not warranted. And yet sometimes strong words need to be uttered. Jeremiah can already hear and see the signs of impending war, in the raising of the standard and the call of the trumpet.

Jeremiah's words call to mind to me the current climate emergency. Those with eyes to see and ears to hear can tell that our present path of burning fossil fuels while enjoying a highly meat-based diet is not sustainable for the planet we live on. We hear the warning cries of scientists and see the impact of ever more frequent extreme weather events on our televisions. Yet human behaviour proves stubbornly resistant to change. We say it is for 'someone else' to alter the way they consume the earth's resources, 'not for me'.

Heavenly Father, you have created this beautiful planet on which we live, yet we fail to share and conserve its resources.
Help us to hear and heed the warning cries, and to play our own part in being the change we yearn to see. Amen.

DAVID WALKER

Silence in heaven

When the Lamb broke the seventh seal, there was silence in heaven for about half an hour. And I saw the seven angels who stand before God, and seven trumpets were given to them. Another angel with a golden censer came and stood at the altar; he was given a great quantity of incense to offer with the prayers of all the saints on the golden altar that is before the throne. And the smoke of the incense, with the prayers of the saints, rose before God from the hand of the angel. Then the angel took the censer and filled it with fire from the altar and threw it on the earth, and there were peals of thunder, rumblings, flashes of lightning, and an earthquake.

The book of Revelation is full of action, often of the most spectacular kind. And yet here, right at the heart of John's description of the end times, we have not merely a short break in the rapid sequence of events, but half an hour of complete silence. It comes at one of the most powerful moments of the book. The last of the seven seals has been broken, and the last seven trumpets are about to sound. Unsurprisingly, it ends in dramatic fashion, with thunder, lightning and an earthquake, but for a full 30 minutes silence reigns. Not that nothing is happening at all. An angel is censing the golden altar, while all the saints join in prayer.

Sometimes, I enjoy being surrounded by noisy and extrovert worship. But it would not serve me as a balanced diet. I need silence too. Indeed, part of our weekday routine is for my wife and I to set aside half an hour for silent prayer before breakfast. It can be one of the most refreshing times of the day. I rejoice that such silent worship is not something confined to earth, but that it forms part of the worshipping life of eternity. For me, it would not truly be heaven if there were no silence.

God of eternity, thank you that your kingdom has space for silence.
Help me so to embrace such silence throughout this earthly life,
that I may be strengthened by it for your service here below,
and likewise prepared for your worship in heaven. Amen.

DAVID WALKER

Acts 8—15

This middle section of Luke's Acts of the Apostles begins with news of serious persecution that threatens the life of the infant church. However, rather than repressing its activities, this persecution triggers a dynamic wave of new missional energy that directly fulfils Jesus' prophecy to his disciples before his Ascension, where he tells them that they will be witnesses not just in Jerusalem, but in Judea, in Samaria and to the ends of the earth (Acts 1:8). At the end of Acts 7 we are left a little shell-shocked by the appalling stoning of Stephen, who was one of the seven (Acts 6:5). He was clearly a highly gifted teacher and evangelist.

Another of the seven is Philip, and he steps on to the stage after Stephen's death. Driven by the wind of the Spirit of God, he now moves out of Jerusalem and preaches in Samaria and also converts a senior Ethiopian official. The gospel is now spreading fast, and the speed of this evangelistic impetus accelerates with the conversion of Saul. Acquiring the new name of Paul, he receives a call to take the good news of Jesus not only to new nations, but to those who have hitherto been deemed religiously unclean: the Gentiles. We will follow him as he embarks on the first of his great missionary journeys.

In the coming days we shall find ourselves joining the likes of Philip, Peter, Paul and Barnabas in the high adventures of this remarkable explosion of evangelistic life that would transform the Roman Empire with the message of the crucified Christ, and which in time would reach the very ends of the earth. It is possible to read these stories simply as admirers of these heroes of faith, applauding their endeavours and lamenting the fact that their experience of courageous and effective evangelism may make ours look pale by comparison. But Luke does not want his readers to be admirers; he wants us to be participants: to treat these ambassadors of Christ as friends and to allow the Holy Spirit of Pentecost to ignite these wonderful stories in our own hearts, so that wherever we may find ourselves, the warmth of them may have a gospel effect on the lives of those around us.

MICHAEL MITTON

Joy in the city

Now those who were scattered went from place to place proclaiming the word. Philip went down to the city of Samaria and proclaimed the Messiah to them. The crowds with one accord listened eagerly to what was said by Philip, hearing and seeing the signs that he did, for unclean spirits, crying with loud shrieks, came out of many who were possessed, and many others who were paralysed or lame were cured. So there was great joy in that city.

Following the violent murder of Stephen, the followers of Christ fled from Jerusalem, a city that was no longer safe for them. You might think they would keep their mouths firmly shut for fear of a similar fate befalling them. However, we find quite the opposite. Five times in this chapter, Luke uses the term 'evangelise' (translated 'proclaiming' in the passage above). No threats manage to stop these people talking about Jesus.

Philip heads for a city in Samaria, and this is a remarkably bold step. The hatred between Jews and Samaritans was well known (see John 4:9). It went back a thousand years, and yet in this hostile setting, Philip speaks to the Samaritan people with a surprising confidence and freedom. In addition to his preaching, he is also used by God to bring healing and deliverance to many Samaritans. The working of such miracles was not confined to the apostles. Any bearer of the gospel could be a channel of God's grace. The story makes clear that even those regarded as heretics and enemies are beloved of God, and can be recipients of his works of wonder. This little story ends with a most beautiful result: there was great joy in the city.

Many of us may feel we are not natural wonder-working evangelists, and therefore can easily brush past a story like this. But it is good from time to time to remind ourselves of the extraordinary life-changing power of the gospel that can break out in the toughest of life circumstances, and which is good news for all people, no matter their race, religion or culture.

What was it that caused those Samaritans to be so full of joy?
How might God want to use you to be a messenger of gospel joy today?

MICHAEL MITTON

Word and Spirit

Now when the apostles at Jerusalem heard that Samaria had accepted the word of God, they sent Peter and John to them. The two went down and prayed for them that they might receive the Holy Spirit (for as yet the Spirit had not come upon any of them; they had only been baptised in the name of the Lord Jesus). Then Peter and John laid their hands on them, and they received the Holy Spirit.

When Luke writes that the Samaritans had 'accepted' the word of God, he is telling us that another stage of evangelisation has happened. The first was on the day of Pentecost when the Jews accepted the gospel (Acts 2:41). The Samaritan's acceptance is the second stage. The third will be the acceptance by the Gentiles (Acts 11:1). At every stage we see this lovely harmony of word and Spirit. The crowd at Pentecost saw evidence of the Spirit on the disciples, and Peter's sermon included reference to the promise of the Spirit (Acts 2:38). And in Acts 11, Peter reports that the Spirit came upon the Gentile Cornelius and his household as he began to speak. Here, the reception of the Spirit comes through the laying on of hands by Peter and John. In passing, we might note that at one time John wanted fire to fall from heaven to burn up the Samaritans (Luke 9:54)!

There has been much argument over the centuries regarding when and how the Holy Spirit is conveyed to the believer. It is likely that Luke's concern in Acts is not to develop a neat theology of the Spirit, but to report something that he sees to be highly significant, which is that we are all in need of the empowering and enlivening presence of the Holy Spirit in our lives. And this is not a gift awarded after months of study or granted to those who are particularly holy. It is a gift for beginners, and it is a gift for any who are humble enough to know they need help. Luke is clear: the presence of the Spirit is crucial for all mission and ministry.

What is your experience of the Holy Spirit? Spend some time consciously receiving his refreshing and empowering presence today.

MICHAEL MITTON

The listening evangelist

[The Ethiopian eunuch] invited Philip to get in and sit beside him. Now the passage of the scripture that he was reading was this: 'Like a sheep he was led to the slaughter, and like a lamb silent before its shearer, so he does not open his mouth'… The eunuch asked Philip, 'About whom, may I ask you, does the prophet say this, about himself or about someone else?' Then Philip began to speak, and starting with this scripture, he proclaimed to him the good news about Jesus.

A key feature of this much-loved story is Philip's impressive willingness and ability to listen. His missionary endeavour in Samaria is interrupted by an angel who gives him a strange commission. With things going so well there, it might have seemed surprising to Philip to be called away to a desert road (Acts 8:26). Yet off he goes, presumably with little clue as to what task will be assigned to him when he gets there.

Once he gets to this desert road he meets a bit of traffic which includes the chariot of a senior official of the distant land of Ethiopia. Philip hears the voice of the Spirit telling him to walk by the chariot (Acts 8:29), and in doing so, he hears the man reading aloud a passage of Isaiah. We can assume Philip had little experience of meeting foreign dignitaries, but nonetheless he manages to gain the official's confidence, for the Ethiopian invites him into his carriage.

The man is puzzled and cannot make head nor tail of this reading. We then get an episode similar to Luke's account of the two friends on the road to Emmaus (Luke 24:13ff). In that story, Jesus is willing to give time to listen to them. In the same way, Philip is willing to ride in the Ethiopian's chariot and listen to his questions.

In his book *Life Together*, Dietrich Bonhoeffer wrote that we must first learn to listen with the ears of God before we proclaim the word of God. Philip demonstrates for us a delightful ability to listen both to God and to people. The most effective evangelism comes from a listening heart.

Think about Bonhoeffer's words.
How might you apply them in your life today?

MICHAEL MITTON

Heroic trust

But Ananias answered, 'Lord, I have heard from many about this man [Saul], how much evil he has done to your saints in Jerusalem, and here he has authority from the chief priests to bind all who invoke your name.' But the Lord said to him, 'Go, for he is an instrument whom I have chosen to bring my name before gentiles and kings and before the people of Israel; I myself will show him how much he must suffer for the sake of my name.'

In chapter 9 we return to the story of the persecutor Saul, who is dramatically converted on the road to Damascus. For much of Luke's book, Saul, who becomes Paul, will take centre stage. But in today's passage we meet a local Christian called Ananias, who is truly heroic. He is presumably a recent convert, and yet we see he has a confident relationship with God in which he feels free to question God's instruction to him. His response to God's command suggests that he feels God doesn't quite appreciate the severity of Saul's violent nature. God does not appear offended by Ananias' cautionary response, but simply tells him to get on with the job.

As if it's not enough to go and knock on the door of the infamous persecutor of Christians, Ananias is also charged with healing the man of blindness, and then delivering a sobering message to him that includes the fact that Saul will experience much suffering. Many of us might well have baulked at this awesome commission. But Ananias is wonderfully faith-filled. He is confident in the power of the gospel to change even the hardest of hearts. He finds Saul, and indeed heals him of his blindness and delivers the divine message to him.

We may come across those whose hearts have been hardened by bitterness, even hatred, as was Saul's. But Ananias would encourage us to always give time to listening to God. What is he saying about that person? No heart is beyond the reach of the transforming love of God.

Is there anyone you know who seems to have a hard heart?
What does God say to you about them?
Imagine how they might be, when they are transformed by Christ.

MICHAEL MITTON

Tabitha, get up!

Now in Joppa there was a disciple whose name was Tabitha… At that time she became ill and died. When they had washed her, they laid her in a room upstairs… When [Peter] arrived, they took him to the room upstairs. All the widows stood beside him, weeping and showing tunics and other clothing that Dorcas had made while she was with them. Peter put all of them outside, and then he knelt down and prayed. He turned to the body and said, 'Tabitha, get up.' Then she opened her eyes, and seeing Peter, she sat up.

Saul makes his way to Jerusalem, and we leave him there for a while as Luke fills us in on some events in the ministry of Peter, who is travelling towards the coast (Acts 9:32). When he gets to Joppa he gets a knock on the door, and two men inform him that a much-loved friend has died. Her name is Tabitha, and she had a reputation for being deeply caring of the poor (v. 36). We then have one of the most touchingly human passages of scripture, where Luke describes so movingly how the grieving friends of Tabitha show Peter the beautiful clothes that she had made (v. 39). And next to this display of her craftsmanship lies the lifeless body of the seamstress.

It is not clear whether the friends' intention of calling Peter is to receive his comfort or to ask him to raise her from death. Peter, however, has a powerful intuition that he must pray for her return to life. He has seen his Master in just such a situation in the home of Jairus (Luke 8:49–55). Following Jesus' example, Peter sends the mourners out of the room, takes hold of the lifeless hand and commands the woman to rise. As with the story of Jairus' daughter, this astounding dead-raising story travels throughout the region.

Stories of literal resurrection such as this are rare in the history of the church, but there is a principle here that is foundational to the gospel. That is, the kingdom of God is about heavenly power encountering vulnerable humanity. It is about the dynamic influence of resurrection life in our broken world.

How can you be a messenger of resurrection life today?

MICHAEL MITTON

The acceptable offering

In Caesarea there was a man named Cornelius, a centurion of the Italian Cohort, as it was called. He was a devout man who feared God with all his household; he gave alms generously to the people and prayed constantly to God. One afternoon at about three o'clock he had a vision in which he clearly saw an angel of God coming in and saying to him, 'Cornelius.' He stared at him in terror and said, 'What is it, Lord?' He answered, 'Your prayers and your alms have ascended as a memorial before God.'

We now move to the coastal city of Caesarea, which is the headquarters of the government of Palestine, and here Luke introduces us to a centurion named Cornelius. A centurion would be the equivalent of a company sergeant-major in a modern army. Lest any readers should have a stereotyped image of a cruel, thick-skinned, pagan centurion, Luke is quick to point out that Cornelius is very different. He is devout, for one thing, which means he had respect for the local religion, and may well have attended synagogue worship. Even though he represented the oppressive occupying power of Rome, he was clearly doing the local community much good. It is to this man that one day an angel calls, and tells him that his prayers and deeds have ascended to heaven as a memorial.

The word 'memorial' is the equivalent to that used in Leviticus 2:2, 9 and 16 for a burnt offering. Perhaps Cornelius knew of Psalm 141:2: 'Let my prayer be counted as incense before you and the lifting up of my hands as an evening sacrifice.' However devout Cornelius was, he was surely not expecting a visit from an angel. And it is very unlikely that he expected to receive such a high complement from heaven for his prayer life and almsgiving.

It is worth reading through the whole of Cornelius' story to see exactly how God honours this centurion's quality of character. Too often we can look at others whom we deem to be far more qualified than us to receive God's appreciation. Cornelius would remind us that all that is needed is a prayerful and generous heart.

How might you develop a prayerful and generous heart?

MICHAEL MITTON

Seeing in a new light

Now while Peter was greatly puzzled about what to make of the vision that he had seen, suddenly the men sent by Cornelius appeared... They called out to ask whether Simon, who was called Peter, was staying there. While Peter was still thinking about the vision, the Spirit said to him, 'Look, three men are searching for you. Now get up, go down, and go with them without hesitation, for I have sent them.' So Peter went down to the men and said, 'I am the one you are looking for; what is the reason for your coming?'

As we read on, we discover that Cornelius is part of an extraordinary revelation that is coming Peter's way. Even though Peter's life has been so transformed by his journey with Christ, he still harbours a prejudice that he believes to be a holy conviction. It is to do with his belief that when it comes to the favour of God, some people are 'in' and some are 'out', and the people who are out are specifically the Gentiles.

But we see some leniency in Peter's conviction, for we read that he is lodging with a tanner while in Joppa (9:43). For strict adherents to the law, those dealing with animal skins were unclean. But more than leniency is required of Peter: he needs to see the world in a whole new way. And his eyes are opened during a time when he was supposed to be praying but had become distracted by his rumbling tummy (v. 10). This distraction of hunger becomes the pathway to a remarkable vision (vv. 11–16). While Peter is puzzling over the meaning of the vision, the Spirit gives him his marching orders to go with the men who have arrived downstairs. Peter discovers the meaning of the vision when he meets Cornelius and hears his story (see Peter's account in Acts 11:1–18).

Few of us have the kind of vision experienced by Peter, but we can have moments when through such things as a dream, a chance meeting, a line of poetry or a moment of deep stillness, we become aware of a truth we have hitherto missed. Such moments are to be treasured.

How might God want to open your eyes today?

MICHAEL MITTON

The Holy Spirit came

While Peter was still speaking, the Holy Spirit fell upon all who heard the word. The circumcised believers who had come with Peter were astounded that the gift of the Holy Spirit had been poured out even on the gentiles, for they heard them speaking in tongues and extolling God. Then Peter said, 'Can anyone withhold the water for baptising these people who have received the Holy Spirit just as we have?' So he ordered them to be baptised in the name of Jesus Christ. Then they invited him to stay for several days.

As Cornelius and his household are converted to Christianity, Peter is also converted to a whole new way of understanding salvation. 'I truly understand that God shows no partiality,' he says (v. 34). Peter's response to all of this is to preach, but he is interrupted by the Spirit, who has had enough of words, and showers the new converts with his joyful gifts. There are still some in the room who think that Gentiles should be denied such things, and they are surprised (and hopefully delighted) when they realise that this is a gift for all, not only those with particular religious credentials.

Had there been doctors of theology and curators of church order present, they might well have protested that the water baptism should come *before* the impartation of the Spirit. And perhaps, while they would be arguing together in a corner of the house, Cornelius and his household would be dancing with Spirit-filled joy in the fountain, with Peter sloshing water all over them!

The story is a wonderful example of how the grace of God, imparted by the Holy Spirit, can joyfully disrupt our neatly controlled doctrines and church practices. It is not that God takes pleasure in any form of chaos. It is simply that God is passionate to free us of anything that binds us and traps us in legalistic lifestyles. One of the Spirit's greatest gifts is freedom. Paul wrote to the Corinthians: 'Where the Spirit of the Lord is, there is freedom' (2 Corinthians 3:17). The Pentecost season is a good time to explore where in our lives we need the freedom of the Spirit.

Where do you need freedom today? Pray for the Spirit to release you.

MICHAEL MITTON

To cleave unto the Lord

And the hand of the Lord was with them: and a great number believed, and turned unto the Lord. Then tidings of these things came unto the ears of the church which was in Jerusalem: and they sent forth Barnabas, that he should go as far as Antioch. Who, when he came, and had seen the grace of God, was glad, and exhorted them all, that with purpose of heart they would cleave unto the Lord… Then departed Barnabas to Tarsus, for to seek Saul.

News of God's acceptance of the Gentiles spreads fast in the church, for in Acts 11:20 we hear of a team from Cyprus and Cyrene embarking on an evangelistic mission to the Gentile city of Antioch. There is clearly still some disquiet in the Jerusalem church about these Gentile converts, so they choose a man called Barnabas to go to Antioch to check all is in order. We have met Barnabas before, in Acts 4:36–37, where we are told his name means 'son of encouragement' (NRSV), and in Acts 9:27, where he vouches for Paul when many could not believe his conversion.

So, Barnabas heads off to check out what's happening in Antioch, and when he gets there he is clearly delighted, for he could see clear evidence of the grace of God at work. He sees that now a great number of Gentiles are becoming believers, and he realises that he is going to need help. And the man who comes to mind is the former persecutor of the church, who was converted near Damascus. There has been no record of Saul for several years, but Barnabas goes and collects him, and thus begins the public ministry of the one who becomes Paul.

Barnabas comes over as a wonderful person, and he seems to have one main message on his heart: to cleave to the Lord with purpose of heart (v. 23). He may well have been a fine teacher, but the impression is that it was the sheer quality of his own devotion to Jesus that inspired others. Every church needs those whose witness is simply demonstrating the winsome beauty of a life devoted to Christ.

What does 'cleaving to the Lord with purpose of heart' mean to you?

MICHAEL MITTON

Peter is at the door!

As soon as [Peter] realised this, he went to the house of Mary… where many had gathered and were praying. When he knocked at the outer gate, a maid named Rhoda came to answer. On recognising Peter's voice, she was so overjoyed that, instead of opening the gate, she ran in and announced that Peter was standing at the gate. They said to her, 'You are out of your mind!' But she insisted that it was so. They said, 'It is his angel.' Meanwhile Peter continued knocking, and when they opened the gate they saw him and were amazed.

The rate of conversions to this new faith was causing some disturbance, so Herod arrests and executes James (12:2). The church must have been appalled at the news of the killing of one of Jesus' closest disciples. Seeing an opportunity to boost his popularity, Herod arrests Peter as well, no doubt with the intention of killing him. But it is a festival, so he has to put Peter in prison until the festival has ended. The Christians must have fully expected Peter to also be put to death.

However, while in prison, Peter experiences something he clearly did not expect to happen: a jail breakout managed by an angel (vv. 7–11). Peter eventually realises that this escape is no vision, but is really happening, and he makes his way to Mary's house, where there is a prayer meeting being held for his release.

We then have one of the most comical passages of scripture, and it is wonderful that Luke has chosen to include this almost farcical scene of the escapee, Peter, hammering on the door, but no one believing it is him! Amid this extraordinary story of supernatural release from prison, we find a regular bit of human comedy, and maybe Luke is keen to remind us that those who found themselves in these stories of miracle and wonder were as human as the rest of us. They knew grief in the death of James. They knew human comedy with Peter at the door. And God was in it all.

Read through the full story (vv. 1–19), and then reflect
on the mix of human and miracle in your own life.

MICHAEL MITTON

Encounters with darkness

But the magician Elymas (for that is the translation of his name) opposed them and tried to turn the proconsul away from the faith. But Saul, also known as Paul, filled with the Holy Spirit, looked intently at him and said, 'You son of the devil, you enemy of all righteousness, full of all deceit and villainy, will you not stop making crooked the straight paths of the Lord? And now listen – the hand of the Lord is against you, and you will be blind for a while, unable to see the sun.'

Chapter 13 marks the beginning of Paul's great missionary journeys. While at Antioch, he and Barnabas are commissioned for their evangelistic task, and their first stop is Cyprus, Barnabas' homeland (Acts 4:36). They go on a preaching tour through the island and come to the western town of Paphos, the base for the Roman proconsul. This proconsul is favourable to Paul and Barnabas, and encourages their mission.

However, typical of his time, this proconsul is intensely superstitious, and he is connected to an occultist whom Luke calls Elymas. This Elymas can sense a real threat from these evangelists, and he knows that if the proconsul takes on this faith, then he will be redundant. Luke now takes this opportunity to tell us that Saul is also called Paul, and this is the name he uses for the rest of his book. Paul, on encountering Elymas, now opens himself to the active influence of the Holy Spirit, and he also looks not just *at* the man, but *into* the man. This combination of spiritual grace and human perceptiveness allows Paul to see the operation of dark powers, and he immediately deals with them. Elymas, who no doubt boasted about being able to see things that others could not, now finds himself sightless. Not surprisingly, the proconsul is converted when he sees such power at work.

What shines clear in Acts is that the followers of Jesus are well equipped to challenge the power of darkness operating in this world. To do so, we need to exercise very discerning listening and seeing, and for that we need the grace of the Holy Spirit.

How might God want to use you to counter the darkness
and proclaim his light?

MICHAEL MITTON

The God of all things

When the crowds saw what Paul had done, they shouted in the Lycaonian language, 'The gods have come down to us in human form!' Barnabas they called Zeus, and Paul they called Hermes... When the apostles Barnabas and Paul heard of it, they tore their clothes and rushed out into the crowd, shouting, 'People, why are you doing this? We are mortals just like you, and we bring you good news, that you should turn from these worthless things to the living God, who made the heaven and the earth and the sea and all that is in them.'

After leaving Cyprus, Paul and Barnabas sail to Asia Minor, and they evangelise in various cities. In today's passage, we read of their experience in Lystra where Luke records Paul's healing of a lame man (14:8–10). The crowd are naturally astonished at this miracle, which causes them to wonder quite what these two foreign visitors are made of.

There was a well-known legend in Lystra that once upon a time, Zeus and Hermes decided to visit Phrygia, and they went in disguise. For some reason none of the townspeople offered them hospitality, except for two peasants. The gods were offended by this rejection and sent a flood to destroy the inhospitable homes, but saved the two peasants. So, when the people of Lystra witness the miracle performed by Paul, they suspect these are the two gods who have visited in disguise again, and they have no intention of offending them this time.

Understandably, Paul and Barnabas protest that they are as human as the rest of them. But then they preach some words ideally suited to a pagan audience. Here, they can't appeal to the scriptures, so they refer instead to the revelation of God in creation. They steer the people's eyes and hearts away from their gods, who have done nothing but create fear in them, to the God who has created all things. This God, they say, is good and wants to bring them much joy (v. 17). It seems the crowd was not entirely convinced (v. 18), though a church is established there (vv. 21–23).

What 'gods' do you observe people worshipping in today's culture?
How would you share God's love with these people?

MICHAEL MITTON

No them and us

After there had been much debate, Peter stood up and said to them, 'My brothers, you know that in the early days God made a choice among you, that I should be the one through whom the gentiles would hear the message of the good news and become believers. And God, who knows the human heart, testified to them by giving them the Holy Spirit, just as he did to us, and in cleansing their hearts by faith he has made no distinction between them and us.'

With the success of the gospel spreading among the Gentiles, questions have started to arise about whether some of the customs and rituals of the old religion should be kept. A key rite of the established religion is that of circumcision, and there is a group of new Christians based in Jerusalem, who have started to travel around stating that circumcision is still necessary for salvation (Acts 15:1).

Paul and Barnabas will have none of this, and they go straight to Jerusalem to discuss the matter with the elders. On arrival, rather than launching into theological or ecclesiastical debate, they simply tell stories of what God has been doing on their travels (v. 4). While most rejoice, some Pharisees present insist that law-keeping is vital for salvation.

So the church leaders meet together, and Peter gives a powerful address. It is his last appearance in Acts. In today's passage we can assume he is referring to his significant dream and the meeting with Cornelius that transformed his thinking. This was probably ten years before, but it is still fresh in Peter's mind.

Four times in Peter's speech he refers to 'us–them' or 'we–they' (vv. 8–11). He is adamant that there must be no divisions created by religious practices. We are getting sight here of a deep conviction growing in the heart of this early church, which Paul would describe as 'There is no longer Jew or Greek… slave or free… male and female' (Galatians 3:28). Religious people can all too easily create rules and systems that serve only to separate them from others.

How do you feel about others who practise their faith
very differently from you? What does God say to you about them today?

MICHAEL MITTON

Human beings after all!

After some days Paul said to Barnabas, 'Come, let us return and visit the brothers and sisters in every city where we proclaimed the word of the Lord and see how they are doing.' Barnabas wanted to take with them John called Mark. But Paul decided not to take with them one who had deserted them in Pamphylia and had not accompanied them in the work. The disagreement became so sharp that they parted company.

It was Barnabas who first ushered Paul into the missionary arena, but he now finds himself in fierce opposition to him over the question of whether his cousin, Mark, should join them in the next stage of the mission. Paul is adamant that he should not.

The incident Paul refers to can be found in Acts 13:13, where, after the mission to Cyprus, Mark leaves them and returns to Jerusalem. We do not know the reason for this, but clearly in Paul's mind it was a desertion of duty. Barnabas, the encourager, takes a far more pastoral role, and determines that Mark can grow strong. Barnabas and Mark do not appear again in Acts, but it seems Mark becomes a close companion of Peter, who calls him his 'son' (1 Peter 5:13). Paul later recognises the growth that happens in Mark, for he refers to him in his letters (Colossians 4:10; Philemon 24; 2 Timothy 4:11). Each reference commends him as a strong and dependable friend.

There is something both admirable and encouraging about the fact that Luke chose to detail this quarrel that broke out between the two prominent missionaries, Paul and Barnabas. He makes no judgement about the conflict, but simply reports it as part of life. Perhaps he is keen to convey that these early Christian pioneers were just as human as the rest of us and, in common with us, they could disagree with each other and fall out. He does not relate this story to sanction quarrelling, but he does make clear that it is not the end of the world. Luke does not set up Paul, Barnabas and Mark as untainted heroes. But he does make clear that none of our human failings are beyond the reach of the grace of God.

How might God transform your failings?

MICHAEL MITTON

Romans 12—16

When considering the theology of Paul's letter to the church in Rome, the image that comes to my mind is a rich fruitcake. Within the first eleven chapters there are several significant ingredients: God's power to save; a world in need; God's free gift; Abraham's faith; Christ and Adam; freedom; sin; law; death; resurrection; Jews and Gentiles; 'in Christ' – to name only a few. While each is necessary and recognisable, Paul skilfully combines all the elements to produce an overall 'cake': God has revealed himself through Jesus and will freely accept anyone from any background who has faith in the death and resurrection of Christ.

To take the metaphor too far, chapters 12—15 focus on how the cake might taste, while chapter 16 introduces the people who first ate it! In other words, Romans 1—11 explore the theory of Christian faith, Romans 12—15 what the theory might look like in practice, and Romans 16 offers a teasing glimpse at members of the church in Rome. The 'icing' is a final blessing.

Over the centuries, many learned scholars have written about Romans. Especially helpful in compiling these studies has been Paula Gooder's book *Phoebe: A story* (Hachette, 2019). The story imagines the church in Rome receiving Paul's letter and invites readers to consider how, in those days, members of the congregation might have come to faith and faced the joys and challenges of Christian discipleship. Two millennia later, a surprising number of issues remain relevant. Over the next two weeks we shall delve into a few of these but, sadly, leave other significant matters untouched.

To make sense of the studies, it would be worth spending a couple of hours reading or listening to the whole letter to the Romans. The danger of reading the set passages and comments in isolation is that suggested actions or prayers become items for the 'to do list'. In a world of soundbites and instant gratification, it is vital to see the practical issues as an outworking of God's mercy to humanity in the life, death and resurrection of Jesus and in the power of the Holy Spirit. For this we need the mind of Christ – the subject of our first study. So dig in and taste the delights the Lord has for you!

LAKSHMI JEFFREYS

Mind and body

I appeal to you therefore, brothers and sisters, on the basis of God's mercy, to present your bodies as a living sacrifice, holy and acceptable to God, which is your reasonable act of worship. Do not be conformed to this age, but be transformed by the renewing of the mind, so that you may discern what is the will of God – what is good and acceptable and perfect.

From the 1980s onwards, society seemed to become obsessed with physical fitness. You could purchase a video (do you remember those?) of someone, often dressed in lycra, showing you how to get the body you dreamed of. During the Covid pandemic, the link between mental and physical well-being was increasingly obvious to everyone, as fitness guru Joe Wicks entered our homes. In fact the well-being industry has grown throughout the 21st century, with online gurus currently enticing their followers to undertake particular disciplines in order to become their best selves.

Paul's message in these verses could not be more different. While fitness videos and modern well-being put the individual at the centre, Paul directs his hearers back to God. In the previous eleven chapters of the letter, Paul has detailed God's mercies in sending Jesus to die for sinful humanity, whether Jew or Gentile, and sending the Holy Spirit to enable us to live as God's redeemed people. As a result of all of this, we are to allow God to transform our thinking – about God, about ourselves and about the world. Life is no longer about being 'the best me' but about becoming the person God created me to be. I live not for myself but in sacrificial worship to God and in service to the world.

Notice that worship involves what we do with our bodies – practical action, putting God and neighbour before ourselves. (Paula Gooder writes movingly about how unbearable these verses could have been for female slaves, who had no choice in how their bodies were sacrificed to and used by male owners.) But the key is how we think and allow God to direct our actions. There is no 'Christian behaviour' unless my mind is focused on Christ.

Gracious God, forgive me for wanting to look like a Christian but conform to society. Please convert my thinking and thereby direct my actions.

LAKSHMI JEFFREYS

Attitude in church

Because of the privilege and authority God has given me, I give each of you this warning: Don't think you are better than you really are. Be honest in your evaluation of yourselves, measuring yourselves by the faith God has given us. Just as our bodies have many parts and each part has a special function, so it is with Christ's body. We are many parts of one body, and we all belong to each other. In his grace, God has given us different gifts for doing certain things well.

How do you think about yourself? As a university student I used to combine poor self-image with the assumption I knew everything! Bible passages about being the body of Christ sent me into a panic, as I imagined myself to be a fungal toenail! Having our minds renewed by God (as we heard yesterday) allows us to see ourselves as we really are and to recognise our place and duty within the church. When we have the mind of Christ, we are better able to discover our part in the body of Christ. In fact, most of the remainder of the letter is about mutual relationships among Christians and how the church operates together. We have a shared purpose – to show and tell people of God's saving love in Jesus Christ – but we need to find out what our particular role is, in order for the purpose to be realised.

If we focus on ourselves or even on the people around us, we can quickly become disheartened or arrogant. Paul reminds us that our gifts come from God and are best employed as we have faith in God – ask him what to do and how – as individuals and alongside one another.

One year a group of people told the Easter story through structured activities at their church. The woman in her 80s captivated her audience of adults and children as she brought alive the events of Palm Sunday, while the business executive beautifully enabled people to enact and understand Jesus washing his disciples' feet. The disparate group became a well-honed body. Would that church was always like this!

---

*Ask God to show you the gifts of people in your church
and your part in Christ's body.*

LAKSHMI JEFFREYS

Attitude in society

Dear friends, never take revenge. Leave that to the righteous anger of God. For the Scriptures say, 'I will take revenge; I will pay them back,' says the Lord. Instead, 'If your enemies are hungry, feed them. If they are thirsty, give them something to drink. In doing this, you will heap burning coals of shame on their heads.' Don't let evil conquer you, but conquer evil by doing good.

Paul quotes scripture to reinforce the radical nature of God's love. Christians are to show the same attitude to one another and in wider society. The sermon on the mount (Matthew 5—7) is full of examples of the extraordinary behaviour Jesus expected of his followers. In the verses preceding today's passage, Paul gives similar commands to bless one's enemies (v. 14), to treat all people with respect, regardless of their status in society (v. 16) and to be at peace with everyone, as far as it is possible (v. 18). (Jesus said peacemakers would be blessed.)

While none of this is easy in practice and everything has to be undergirded by prayer (v. 12), the instruction never to take revenge is probably hardest of all. Getting back at the person who has damaged us in some way seems almost instinctual. Indeed, the Old Testament law, which said 'an eye for an eye', was to ensure the desire for revenge was managed. Whether employing 'revenge porn' after a breakdown in relationship or demanding impossibly punitive reparations of the losing side after a war, vengeful behaviour results in further evil.

In tomorrow's reading, Paul will explain how Christians should relate to the ruling authorities and follow the laws of the land. At the same time, while we are not to take revenge, Christians are to work for justice and fight evil. The difference is that we are never to belittle or demean another person, regardless of what they have done. We are to condemn what is wrong and show kindness to the perpetrator. As we treat other people with respect and dignity, we remind them (and ourselves) of the God in whose image we are created. He will do the rest.

On the cross, Jesus asked his Father to forgive those who had crucified him – and then he died. Reflect on how costly Christian love is.

LAKSHMI JEFFREYS

Attitude to authority

Let every person be subject to the governing authorities; for there is no authority except from God, and those authorities that exist have been instituted by God. Therefore whoever resists authority resists what God has appointed, and those who resist will incur judgement. For rulers are not a terror to good conduct, but to bad. Do you wish to have no fear of the authority? Then do what is good, and you will receive its approval, for it is God's agent for your good.

At a graduation ceremony, two recipients of honorary degrees made speeches. After the first erudite talk, the second individual addressed the new graduates: 'I can't follow that, so I shall say one thing: the world is being run by cartoon characters – you do better!' The reported conduct of many politicians and other leaders can add weight to that cynical comment.

Did Paul really intend us to be subject to our rulers when their decisions and actions so often appear questionable, laughable or even dangerous? It is worth remembering that Paul was writing while Nero was the Roman emperor. Even before he began to persecute Christians, Nero's corruption was well documented. Paul would never condone such behaviour, and in Philippi he called the rulers to account when they unjustly imprisoned him. So Paul's command needs to be unpacked carefully and in context.

The Bible is full of stories of corrupt leaders – Nebuchadnezzar of Babylon, for example, followed a long tradition of rulers who insisted on being worshipped as gods. Yet in each case, God used the authority figure to further his purposes. From the beginning of creation, God has sought to bring order out of chaos. All national, international and civic authorities want to avoid chaos – at least on their watch. As a result, Christians should be subject to laws that outlaw murder, theft and other misdemeanours that disrupt relationships. We are citizens of the kingdom of heaven and behave accordingly. Sometimes rulers demand evil practices – racial segregation, persecution of a people group, etc. – and quote these verses. Then Christians need to remember whom we ultimately serve and make difficult choices.

Pray for wisdom for Christians living under oppressive regimes,
and pray for civic, national and international leaders.

LAKSHMI JEFFREYS

Attitude to taxes

For the same reason you also pay taxes, for the authorities are God's agents, busy with this very thing. Pay to all what is due to them: taxes to whom taxes are due, revenue to whom revenue is due, respect to whom respect is due, honour to whom honour is due. Owe no one anything, except to love one another, for the one who loves another has fulfilled the law.

I have yet to meet anyone who enjoys paying their taxes! We are aware that money is required for public services, road maintenance, education, welfare and other aspects of life we easily take for granted. We may differ in our views on what proportion of income should be taxed and who should be exempt, but most people recognise some form of tax on revenue as necessary. Once again, Paul offers a positive perspective on what was probably a corrupt system: just as we recognised yesterday that leaders in society are given their authority by God, so civil servants and others who work for the state are God's servants.

At best, anyone who works for the common good, seeking the welfare of others beyond themselves, is demonstrating the values of the kingdom of God. All human systems are flawed, since every human is a sinner (remind yourself of Romans 1—3), yet Christians are nonetheless encouraged to recognise state authorities as under God's authority and submit accordingly.

Simply paying the correct amount of tax and showing respect to officials because they are doing their job can have unexpected consequences. Some years ago, the friend of a friend realised he was not paying enough tax. After numerous letters and phone conversations, he was on first name terms with several officials. They had rarely encountered anyone who wanted to *increase* their tax bill, nor were they used to dealing with a persistent customer who was unfailingly polite and courteous. During the many weeks he spent pursuing his goal, he shared his Christian faith as the basis of all he was doing. Perhaps this is an unusual example of love fulfilling the law.

Jesus said: 'Give therefore to Caesar the things that are Caesar's,
and to God the things that are God's' (Matthew 22:21).
How do you feel about that?

LAKSHMI JEFFREYS

Day and night

Besides this, you know what time it is, how it is now the moment for you to wake from sleep. For salvation is nearer to us now than when we became believers; the night is far gone; the day is near. Let us then throw off the works of darkness and put on the armour of light; let us walk decently as in the day, not in revelling and drunkenness, not in illicit sex and licentiousness, not in quarrelling and jealousy. Instead, put on the Lord Jesus Christ, and make no provision for the flesh, to gratify its desires.

A head teacher became aware of disparaging comments about the school being posted by a parent on social media. The parent involved had been supportive of the school in the past and there was no obvious reason for the change of tone. As the head teacher examined the posts, he discovered they had been sent after midnight. He had an image in his mind of an intoxicated person splurging in ways they would never speak during the day. Inviting the parent into his office, the head teacher indicated the comments and said, 'Posting on social media when you have had a few drinks doesn't do anyone any good. You are better than this.'

Jesus will come again, and we need to be ready. The challenge is that we live in 'in-between' times. In Romans 8, Paul reminded Christians that the Holy Spirit would empower them, even while creation groans, waiting for salvation to be fully realised. And nothing, anywhere at any time, can separate believers from the love of God in Christ. As a result, with our minds renewed and transformed (12:2), we are encouraged to live differently from those around us. Our true home is in heaven and we can practise living this reality, even if our heavenly dwelling is not obvious. The daily choices to ensure we are in the light of Christ can feel like battles, hence the armour. The passage makes sense when we read verses 8–10 about what love looks like; what Jesus looked like; what heaven will be like. Let us rehearse now for eternal life!

Reflect on your words and actions over the past week.
Repent where necessary and ask Jesus to lead you into the day.

LAKSHMI JEFFREYS

Weak and strong

Welcome those who are weak in faith… Some believe in eating anything, while the weak eat only vegetables. Those who eat must not despise those who abstain, and those who abstain must not pass judgement on those who eat, for God has welcomed them. Who are you to pass judgement on slaves of another?… Let all be fully convinced in their own minds. Those who… eat, eat for the Lord, since they give thanks to God, while those who abstain, abstain for the Lord and give thanks to God.

The church in Rome was full of people from different backgrounds and traditions. We shall meet some of them later in these studies. In this passage, Paul is picking up on a significant theme earlier in the letter (especially chapters 9—11): Christ died for everyone, whether Jew or Gentile.

This will be spelled out in later verses but the current crisis involves food laws. For Jewish believers, eating certain things on special days and avoiding particular food, especially meat offered to idols or not prepared in an approved manner, was essential to their worship of God. While they knew, in theory, that Christ had abolished such requirements, it was hard to give up what had become part of their identity as God's people. Meanwhile, other believers would not have such concerns, either because they were Gentiles or they had come to terms with a new life in Christ. These 'strong' Christians were not to patronise the 'weak' believers. (Do read the whole passage to understand Paul's argument.)

It is human nature to associate with people who are similar to us and to be wary of those who are significantly different. The church, Paul contends, has no room for such division. Instead, we are to view one another in relation to God, not ourselves. Food and special days are not central to Jesus' life, death and resurrection – the means of salvation. Instead, the attitudes of thankfulness to God and respecting one another as fellow believers are vital. Once again, thinking needs to be transformed. Over the next couple of days we shall discover further what it means for Christians to accept one another in Christ.

Pray for people who express Christian faith differently from you.
How can you become God's servants alongside one another?

LAKSHMI JEFFREYS

Accountable to God

We do not live to ourselves, and we do not die to ourselves. If we live, we live to the Lord, and if we die, we die to the Lord; so then, whether we live or whether we die, we are the Lord's. For to this end Christ died and lived again, so that he might be Lord of both the dead and the living. Why do you pass judgement… why do you despise your brother or sister? For we will all stand before the judgement seat of God.

One of the central messages of Paul's letter to the Romans is that no one can earn God's love. In Romans 3:21–25, Paul explains how Jesus' death on the cross and resurrection from the dead is the means of people being made right with God (justified), despite the universal nature of sin (putting self before God). In this section, Paul reminds the Romans that God will, through the risen Lord Jesus, judge everyone on judgement day. Each of us will be called to account for our own thoughts, words and deeds – and no one else's.

You might have noticed that following any conflict, whether workers going on strike, nations at war with each other or even a breakdown in personal relationships, the news and other media will take sides, polarising issues and losing sight of the opponent as a person. We are constantly tempted to put ourselves in the right and someone else in the wrong. We look at 'the other' in relation to ourselves.

The conflict in the church was about religious practice, leading one person to condemn another because of their views on food or special days. Once again, Paul's approach flies in the face of contemporary society: his and ours. Paul reminded his hearers that their opinions of themselves and one another did not matter in the least. After all, God has accepted me and the other person; Christ died and was raised from death for them and for me; each member of the church is my brother or sister and all of us will stand together before the judgement seat of God.

Reflect: rather than saying, 'They are wrong,' try,
'I disagree with them and Christ died for them and for me.'

LAKSHMI JEFFREYS

Kingdom life

For the kingdom of God is not food and drink but righteousness and peace and joy in the Holy Spirit. The one who serves Christ in this way is acceptable to God and has human approval… Everything is indeed clean, but it is wrong to make someone stumble by what you eat; it is good not to eat meat or drink wine or do anything that makes your brother or sister stumble. Hold the conviction that you have as your own before God. Blessed are those who have no reason to condemn themselves because of what they approve.

Having shown the church how to see each other's practices in the light of Christ's death and resurrection, Paul continues to instruct the church on how to relate to one another.

If the comments to the 'weak' were directed at Jewish believers (see Saturday's notes), the 'strong' were probably Gentile Christians. These people might have come from more liberal-minded backgrounds, possibly rejoicing in the freedom to worship with others, regardless of status (many of them could have been slaves or former slaves) or other differences. Their ease of conscience, compared with the strict protocol of Jewish believers, might have caused affront. (Some of the Gentile eating habits might have seemed akin to paganism.) So Paul helped them understand that Christ's rule – the kingdom of God – was not about eating, drinking or other similar actions. Jesus called his followers to live at peace with one another. Members of the church should put aside personal preference if it offended someone else.

This has personal resonance. When I was at college, I was invited to share something of my Hindu background. With my parents' permission, I borrowed some of the idols from the shrine in their home. Most of the students saw the idols as I did, having no spiritual power or significance to Christians. Since there were others who felt uncomfortable with idols in the room, we managed the session so that everyone could take part as they felt able. What mattered most was that we were sisters and brothers in Christ.

'Blessed are the peacemakers' (Matthew 5:9). What is the difference between peacemaking and either peacekeeping or compromise? Are there particular challenges to being a peacemaker among Christians?

LAKSHMI JEFFREYS

Following Christ

We who are strong ought to put up with the failings of the weak and not to please ourselves. Each of us must please our neighbour for the good purpose of building up the neighbour. For Christ did not please himself... For whatever was written in former days was written for our instruction, so that by steadfastness and by the encouragement of the scriptures we might have hope. May the God of steadfastness and encouragement grant you to live in harmony with one another, in accordance with Christ Jesus, so that together you may with one voice glorify the God and Father of our Lord Jesus Christ.

In these verses, Paul offers a masterclass in using the Old Testament to show how Jesus was the Messiah and therefore, how we should behave as his disciples. Why should the 'strong' bear with the 'weak' in what seem like their foibles in worship? Why should they not seek to please themselves but instead to build up their neighbour? Because this is how Jesus was.

Quoting from Psalm 69, Paul reminds his hearers that God's strength and power have always been shown through weakness. God's people were small and insignificant in the ancient Near East, to demonstrate that God chose them and worked through them. The cross, an instrument of torture and death, was the means by which God saved the world. Jesus' death demonstrated that even the Messiah did not please himself, so his followers cannot. We have the gospel stories to see further examples of Jesus choosing to serve and not to be served, washing his disciples' feet – even of those who would betray, deny and abandon him. But these build on the picture God has offered from the beginning of a fallen world in need of restoration, which will happen at the end of time.

It is so easy to forget we are part of an eternal plan and to lose sight of the church as the body of Christ, called to unity in Christ. By meditating on the Bible, we are able to rediscover our true purpose and regain perspective on who we are alongside one another. We thereby have hope to continue in the time between Christ's resurrection and the final judgement.

Pray Paul's prayer for your church.

LAKSHMI JEFFREYS

Jews and Gentiles

Welcome one another, therefore, just as Christ has welcomed you, for the glory of God. For I tell you that Christ has become a servant of the circumcised… in order that he might confirm the promises given to the ancestors and that the gentiles might glorify God for his mercy. As it is written, 'Therefore I will confess you among the gentiles and sing praises to your name'… and again Isaiah says, 'The root of Jesse shall come, the one who rises to rule the gentiles; in him the gentiles shall hope.'

Many years ago, over lunch with a family after church, I was invited to share how I came to faith from a Hindu background. An eight-year-old sighed at the end: 'I wish I had a story of conversion.' Inspired by the Holy Spirit, I reminded her of how her parents had prayed for her since before she was born and the privilege she had of being raised in a loving Christian home. Now she and I were in the same church and could share our experiences of God with one another and the wider world, growing together and learning from each other to God's glory.

We are all different from one another and, although we are one in Christ, our background and history shape us. Paul reminds the Jewish believers what was said by Moses, the prophets and in the Psalms about the Messiah. He would be a son of David, serving God's people, and Son of God, ruling at God's right hand. Crucially, his mission would be to the Gentiles as well as the Jews, foretold by the prophets, so that all may glorify God.

Regardless of our background, history, family or anything else by which we might choose to define ourselves, it is Christ who welcomes us and calls us to welcome one another. Differences in ideas and interpretation will remain, but we shall abound with hope as we build on the true foundations of our faith.

Pray and learn Romans 15:13:
'May the God of hope fill you with all joy and peace in believing,
so that you may abound in hope by the power of the Holy Spirit.'

LAKSHMI JEFFREYS

Money matters

I am going to Jerusalem… for Macedonia and Achaia were pleased to share their resources with the poor among the saints… They were pleased to do this, and indeed they owe it to them, for if the gentiles have come to share in their spiritual blessings, they ought also to be of service to them in material things. So, when I have… delivered to them what has been collected, I will set out by way of you to Spain, and I know that when I come to you, I will come in the fullness of the blessing of Christ.

We have omitted verses in which Paul indicates his longing to see his brothers and sisters in Rome, even if this is only a stopover on route from Jerusalem to Spain, as he continues his mission to share the gospel. Instead we shall glance at that most controversial of subjects – money.

For some reason, at least in part a famine predicted by Agabus (Acts 11:27–30), Christians in Judea were in dire need of financial resources. Paul was always at pains to state his mission was to Gentiles, and the church in Jerusalem had been less than supportive of Paul's ministry. Yet he had encouraged relatively wealthy Gentile churches in Macedonia and Achaia to give generously in aid of their Jewish brethren. His reasoning is that the gospel came from the Jews to the Gentiles, so here was a way for the Gentiles to give something back, part of the debt they owe (chapter 11).

I find it fascinating, in this context, that the strong are supporting the weak. It is also important to be aware of the personal danger for Paul. His former friends from the synagogue who had not become Christians would probably hate him, seeing him as a traitor to the faith. Then there was the practical issue of carrying not a bank card or smartphone, nor even paper money, but coins. It is no wonder that later in this chapter Paul asks for prayer, not merely for the offering but primarily that he would be faithful in his mission and ministry.

Consider how our churches would feel about giving to people in need who had opposed our ministry? To whom is God generous?

LAKSHMI JEFFREYS

Individuals matter

I commend to you our sister Phoebe, a deacon of the church at Cenchreae… Greet Prisca and Aquila… also the church in their house. Greet my beloved Epaenetus… Mary… Andronicus and Junia… Ampliatus… Urbanus… Stachys… Apelles… those who belong to the family of Aristobulus… Herodion… those in the Lord who belong to the family of Narcissus… Tryphaena and Tryphosa… Persis… Rufus… and greet his mother… Greet Asyncritus, Phlegon, Hermes, Patrobas, Hermas, and the brothers and sisters who are with them… Philologus, Julia, Nereus and his sister, and Olympas, and all the saints who are with them.

If you are anything like me, you will have both rolled your eyes and been intrigued by speeches made at film or television award ceremonies. The winner, barely able to hold back tears, gushes with gratitude to parents, drama teacher and other seemingly random individuals, as well as coworkers in the industry. (I have yet to discover the role of the 'key grip'!) Paul's 24 named individuals, as well as a sister, a mother and various other family groups, is probably longer than most lists of people thanked when a trophy is won. At the same time, there is no doubting the sincerity of his love for them.

While there are questions about who these individuals were, there is still much we can learn about the church in Rome. They were expected to receive Phoebe, a woman possibly of wealth and influence, with warm hospitality. A few names are of Jewish origin, but most are Gentile, which is to be expected given the content of the letter. There appears to be a mixture of slaves and free men and women, demonstrating the radical nature of the Christian community, where no one has higher or lower status than anyone else. The number and nature of women leaders is striking, particularly Junia, a female apostle, who might well have met the risen Lord Jesus.

But what I love most is how Paul describes the various people: fellow workers, hard workers, fellow prisoners, the Lord's chosen, in the Lord, my dear friend, my relative, like a mother to me: a body of different parts working together.

Ask God to give you the ability to see and treat brothers and sisters in Christ as Paul described his – beloved fellow-workers in the Lord.

LAKSHMI JEFFREYS

The end!

Now to God who is able to strengthen you according to my gospel and the proclamation of Jesus Christ, according to the revelation of the mystery that was kept secret for long ages but is now disclosed, and through the prophetic writings is made known to all the gentiles, according to the command of the eternal God, to bring about the obedience of faith – to the only wise God, through Jesus Christ, to whom be the glory forever! Amen.

A doxology is a carefully constructed ending to a letter which has been written to be read aloud in different settings. It is not Paul's equivalent of 'Best wishes' or 'Yours sincerely'. This doxology is exquisitely composed to reinforce the themes.

The letter and the doxology begin with God's power and strength to sustain people who have faith in him. The gospel of God, detailed in the first eight chapters, is now Paul's good news to proclaim. Jesus Christ has been revealed, once a secret, now seen in his fullness as the means of salvation for Gentiles as well as the people of God in the Old Testament. The prophets wrote of a Messiah not simply for Israel but for a new Israel, encompassing all people in the world who obey God in faith. (Note Paul's reliance on scripture and passion for evangelism.)

This was all planned by God from the very beginning. And this God is the only wise God – a shock in the ancient world, where wisdom was coveted and sought in various places. Throughout the letter, Paul has shown his God to be the creator of the world and redeemer through Jesus. Indeed, Paul wrote a hymn to wisdom in chapter 11 – the only wise God showed his wisdom through the cross. Finally, Jesus is wisdom personified and with God is glorified forever.

So ends Paul's letter to the Romans and our studies on the final chapters. My prayer for you and for myself is that we constantly reflect on God's plan for salvation through Jesus' life, death on the cross and resurrection, and marvel that we have a part to play, alongside our sisters and brothers in Christ. May we thereby, in our thoughts words and actions, give glory to God.

Amen and amen!

LAKSHMI JEFFREYS

Father God

 I have been actively involved in the church's ministry of healing ever since I was ordained over 40 years ago, and in particular since I began working at a charity called The Christian Heal ing Mission. As you might expect, we adopted the logical approach of attending to the needs of those who came to us and lifting them up in prayer. However, over the years, we began to take a different approach. Rather than beginning our times of prayer by focusing on the presenting needs, we sought to shift people's gaze on to the love of Father God for his children.

The reason for this is that we discovered that our visitors' perception of the nature of God directly impacted the way they approached him and how honest they were willing to be. If they felt that he was uncaring, for example, they were less likely to bring the personal details of their lives to him with any confidence of his desire to touch them. Similarly, if they believed that God had high standards and expected his people to live up to them, they were not so readily going to bring all their weaknesses to him.

As well as this, we found that many of our visitors tended to develop their image of God according to their own experiences in life. Sadly this was often negative if they had grown up with a father figure who was either absent, unkind, controlling or even abusive.

So for these reasons we began to change the way we prayed for people and always began our prayer times with a clear focus on Father God's love for his children. It made a huge difference! This same focus can also be seen at the very heart of Jesus' ministry. He was the purest reflection of the Father's love, so by encouraging us to look at him he was showing us a new way to see God.

Over the next two weeks, I invite you to look at some of the astounding passages in the Bible which speak about the nature of Father God and his love for each of us. I hope that you will allow his love to touch you afresh and that this will open up new treasures for you.

JOHN RYELAND

Learning from Jesus

Philip said to him, 'Lord, show us the Father, and we will be satisfied.' Jesus said to him, 'Have I been with you all this time, Philip, and you still do not know me? Whoever has seen me has seen the Father. How can you say, 'Show us the Father'? Do you not believe that I am in the Father and the Father is in me? The words that I say to you I do not speak on my own, but the Father who dwells in me does his works.'

Many people claim to believe in God, but what is God like? Does what you say or sing about God accurately reflect what you really believe in your heart? Some people imagine that God is watching them carefully and noting their every failing, while others assume that he is a generally benevolent figure, happy to bless those who do good but less so with those who have lapsed.

Whatever your thinking, Jesus challenges us to move beyond our own experiences and feelings. His declaration that whoever has seen him has seen the Father prompts us to consider more fully what he has revealed to us, that by looking at him we will learn more about the Father as well.

First, Jesus reveals himself as a friend of sinners. He certainly preached repentance, but rather than hammering it home, his message was conveyed through a demonstration of love, leaving each person free to respond as they wished.

Second, Jesus is full of compassion, longing to bring healing to those who were sick. You may feel that the healing ministry of the church today lacks the power that flowed through Jesus, but even if this is true, it cannot be because God has changed his mind or hardened his heart.

Third, Jesus demonstrated the incredible depth of the Father's love for each of us. Jesus told us that the love he and his Father shared might also be in us so that we would know the extent of the Father's love for us personally (John 17:26).

What is your honest picture of Father God – not what you say or sing but what you really believe? Spend some time considering Jesus and see whether he challenges your thinking.

JOHN RYELAND

The kingdom of God

'Pray then in this way: Our Father in heaven, may your name be revered as holy. May your kingdom come. May your will be done on earth as it is in heaven. Give us today our daily bread. And forgive us our debts, as we also have forgiven our debtors. And do not bring us to the time of trial, but rescue us from the evil one.'

I suspect that we are all accustomed to the phrase 'The kingdom of God', something we might define as the outworking of God's heart among us. But whose kingdom are we talking about? Yes, it is God's kingdom, but can we be a bit more specific? When Jesus taught this prayer to those who were listening, he was addressing the Father – 'Our Father in heaven'. So it is the kingdom and rule of the Father that we are talking about, not even the kingdom of Jesus, although he made his Father's values his own.

This brings us right back to the wonder of the Father's love for us. This prayer, which we call the Lord's Prayer, reflects the heart of Father God for us. It reveals his desire to provide for us and protect us, and his longing for us to receive and pass on forgiveness. I have heard some people say they find it easier to pray to Jesus, as they feel he is more approachable than the Father, whom they perceive as somewhat austere and forbidding. But by teaching us this prayer, Jesus reveals the desperately caring nature of our heavenly Father. He is a Father who wants the very best for us and is willing to intervene to bring that about.

This is such a key revelation about our Father God. Rather than a demanding figure watching from on high as his children struggle and suffer, he is our intervening Father who longs for us to turn to him so that he can be active in bringing about his purposes in our lives.

Take a few moments to say the Lord's Prayer slowly,
and as you do so, try to catch the sense that this is a prayer
directly to the Father who loves you and is willing to act on your behalf.

JOHN RYELAND

Getting started

And whenever you pray, do not be like the hypocrites, for they love to stand and pray in the synagogues and at the street corners, so that they may be seen by others. Truly I tell you, they have received their reward. But whenever you pray, go into your room and shut the door and pray to your Father who is in secret, and your Father who sees in secret will reward you.

I must confess that sometimes I find myself listening to who it is that most people speak to when they pray. In my opinion, most people address their prayers to 'Lord'. There is nothing wrong with this – and thankfully God hears all our prayers – yet Jesus' words instruct us to talk to 'Father' when we pray.

It is not as if prayer is like sending an email, where one mistake in the address sends it to the rubbish bin, so why is Jesus so keen for us to grasp this? Perhaps he is inviting us to begin our times of prayer by reminding ourselves of the beautiful relationship to which we have been called, children of our heavenly Father. Sometimes I hear debates about whether we should begin prayer with praise, confession or some other idea, yet Jesus seems to be saying that prayer begins with something else entirely – relationship.

So how can we develop this relationship? A good starting point is to simply repeat the words 'Father God', maybe in time with our breathing, allowing us to focus on the personal nature of prayer. It does not take long to do this, just enough time to lift our eyes off our own issues and prayer requests and fix them firmly on our loving heavenly Father. In other words, it is not just a matter of saying our prayers, but rather allowing them to be shared in this intimate relationship of love.

At this point, why not pause and say the word 'Father' to yourself as you breathe in and out. Repeat this for a minute or two without consciously articulating any prayer request, and only once you have done this, go on to talk to him about what is on your heart. Afterwards, consider whether this made any difference to your prayers.

JOHN RYELAND

Family relationships

Jesus said to her, 'Mary!' She turned and said to him in Hebrew, 'Rabbouni!' (which means Teacher). Jesus said to her, 'Do not touch me, because I have not yet ascended to the Father. But go to my brothers and say to them, "I am ascending to my Father and your Father, to my God and your God."'

The difference between Jesus and us is all too apparent, and while we are called to grow into his likeness and be like him, we may despair at the thought of how long that process might take. This can lead us to conclude that there is very little of Jesus to which we can aspire.

Yet the words in today's verses reveal something amazing about the nature of our relationship with God the Father. It is like the relationship that Jesus had with him, because we share the same Father. To take this a step further, an additional benefit of being a child of God is that we have Jesus as a brother. Perhaps we can learn more about the fatherhood of God by looking at this brotherhood of Jesus.

First, the intimacy of Jesus' relationship with Father God is attainable to us all but, like Jesus, we probably need to seek it by trying to do the Father's will and spending time with him. The Father has adopted us as his children, so we already have a relationship with him, but the question is whether we are pursuing the intimacy of that relationship?

Second, we have a brother who has done everything he can to help us discover this relationship. The visual image of this in the New Testament is the tearing of the temple curtain, which represented the barrier between God and his people (see Matthew 27:51). When it was torn, it symbolised a new intimacy between God and his people. Thanks to the action of Jesus, the intimacy that he enjoyed with his Father is now available to us.

Take a few minutes to focus on the words 'The Father of our Lord Jesus Christ, and my Father'. As you do so, catch a sense of wonder at the immense privilege of sharing in the same glorious relationship that was so important for Jesus.

JOHN RYELAND

Copying Jesus

He took with him Peter and James and John and began to be distressed and agitated. And he said to them, 'My soul is deeply grieved, even to death; remain here, and keep awake.' And going a little farther, he threw himself on the ground and prayed that, if it were possible, the hour might pass from him. He said, 'Abba, Father, for you all things are possible; remove this cup from me, yet not what I want but what you want.'

Mark's account of Jesus in the garden of Gethsemane is so full of emotion. He begins by sharing the extent of Jesus' desolation with the words, 'My soul is deeply grieved, even to death' (v. 34). The situation and the darkness around him is almost overwhelming.

What is so striking is that instead of trying to cast out the darkness or deny it, he turns to his Father and uses a word that reveals their relationship – 'Abba'. This is the word a child might use for their Father, but the fact that Jesus uses it means that it is not a childish word. It is a word that reveals the trust and dependence of a child with their parent. It is the same word that Paul tells us the Holy Spirit is whispering within each of us (Galatians 4:6; Romans 8:15), keeping alive that same intimacy with the Father that Jesus enjoyed.

We too can use this word 'Abba' in prayer. There is something profound in using the same word that Jesus used to address the same Father that he addressed, and to know that we are called into the same intimacy that the Father and Jesus shared. We might be fearful that such intimacy seems too casual or that it lacks an appropriate sense of awe, but Jesus demonstrates that intimacy and awe are not mutually exclusive. The obedience that he showed to his Father, with whom he enjoyed the most intimate of relationships, is an example we are called to follow.

Take a few moments to imagine Jesus praying and addressing his Father as 'Abba', and then whisper that same word 'Abba' yourself.
Try to sense your heavenly Father's longing for the same intimacy with you that he had with Jesus.

JOHN RYELAND

Discovering intimacy

For this reason I bow my knees before the Father, from whom every family in heaven and on earth takes its name. I pray that, according to the riches of his glory, he may grant that you may be strengthened in your inner being with power through his Spirit, and that Christ may dwell in your hearts through faith, as you are being rooted and grounded in love.

We all have a relationship with God the Father – whether it is close and intimate or somewhat distant – so let us give some thought to what sort of relationship we should have and how we can achieve it.

We are invited to enter a relationship with Father God that is similar to the one that Jesus enjoyed, a relationship of intimacy. So how do we find this? The verses from today's reading open a door for us – relationship comes by kneeling!

Traditionally, the word 'kneeling' suggests kneeling in prayer, but when this letter was written the most common postures for prayer were standing or lying prostrate. Kneeling was associated more with submission. At this point, intimacy with the Father might seem to be less attractive! However, submission need not be perceived as negative, like submitting to an authoritarian figure, but rather submitting to the truth of God's love.

This is certainly good news, but sadly it is far from easy. When circumstances seem to be stacked against us and things seem to keep going wrong so that we cannot sense the presence of God, we may well be tempted to wonder whether he loves us at all. But these are also the times when we need to return to the truth of his love in submission. Rather than listening to our feelings and wondering why God seems distant or against us, we would do better to resolve to follow him and put our trust in his deep and unfailing love for us.

As you begin a time of prayer, take some time to submit to the Father's love. Come before him declaring the truth that you are his adopted child, loved by him so much that he gave Jesus for you. Fight off any feelings that this does not apply to you and stay in that place of his love.

JOHN RYELAND

The top priority

The seventy-two returned with joy, saying, 'Lord, in your name even the demons submit to us!' He said to them, 'I watched Satan fall from heaven like a flash of lightning. Indeed, I have given you authority to tread on snakes and scorpions and over all the power of the enemy, and nothing will hurt you. Nevertheless, do not rejoice at this, that the spirits submit to you, but rejoice that your names are written in heaven.'

Jesus had commissioned 72 followers to go out and minister in his name. They returned amazed at what they had seen and experienced: even demons had responded to them. It is Jesus' reply that is the most telling part of the story. He encouraged them not to rejoice at the effects of their ministry, but because their names were written in heaven.

We have been looking at our relationship with Father God, and while Jesus does not mention the Father in this passage, what he said is so relevant. What is it that causes us to rejoice? The disciples were encouraged not to rejoice at what they saw but in what God had done for them. It is so easy for us to equate the state of our relationship with God with the extent to which our prayers are answered or how he uses us – but what do we do when our prayers seem to go unanswered? It can lead us to feel that somehow our relationship is at fault because of what God may or may not be doing. Whereas if we take these words of Jesus seriously, and make our relationship with him the key issue, we are less likely to be knocked off course if our prayers appear to be unanswered.

Perhaps one of the best ways we can begin to focus on that relationship is to remind ourselves daily of the truth that we are children of Father God, chosen, loved and set apart for relationship with him.

As you begin to pray, rather than looking over the past day or thinking about your future plans, begin by reminding yourself of who you are – a child of the Father, so loved that he gave Jesus for you and so cherished that he longs for relationship with you.

JOHN RYELAND

Amazing love

'Father, I desire that those also, whom you have given me, may be with me where I am, to see my glory, which you have given me because you loved me before the foundation of the world. Righteous Father, the world does not know you, but I know you, and these know that you have sent me. I made your name known to them, and I will make it known, so that the love with which you have loved me may be in them, and I in them.'

This is an amazing statement about the depth of the Father's love for us. The whole of John 17 is a prayer that Jesus prayed to his Father. In it, Jesus prays for himself, his mission, his disciples, and finally he turns his thoughts to those who will believe because of the message of the disciples – that's us!

At the end of his prayer, Jesus reveals that one of his key aims was to reveal Father God's nature to us, so that the love the Father had for him might also be in us. In other words, by revealing what God was like, Jesus hoped that we would discover the depth of God's love for us.

There can be a big difference between the words on our lips and what we believe in our hearts, and when we consider God's love for us it is no different. Perhaps this is not surprising – to be loved by the Father just as Jesus was loved is beyond our comprehension.

The Father's love for Jesus was verbalised at his baptism: 'And a voice came from the heavens, "You are my Son, the Beloved; with you I am well pleased"' (Mark 1:11). If we are loved just as Jesus was loved, then those words that the Father spoke over Jesus are also words he would love us to apply to ourselves – we are his beloved sons and daughters, and he delights in us.

Take a moment to focus on the truth that the love the Father has for Jesus is the same as his love for you – that you are indeed his beloved child and he delights in you. Make it personal and try to let this truth sink deeper into your heart.

JOHN RYELAND

The wonder of being adopted

For all who are led by the Spirit of God are children of God. For you did not receive a spirit of slavery to fall back into fear, but you received a spirit of adoption. When we cry, 'Abba! Father!' it is that very Spirit bearing witness with our spirit that we are children of God, and if children, then heirs: heirs of God and joint heirs with Christ, if we in fact suffer with him so that we may also be glorified with him.

The original recipients of this letter would probably have understood adoption slightly differently to us. Generally, we understand it to be the legal provision of new parents and a new home for children, whereas in the culture of the time, a child was frequently adopted as an heir to an estate and title. However we see it, adoption profoundly changes an individual's permanent status. Once adopted, they are not invited to stay with a new family for a few days and then return to their previous existence, but rather to take their place there and consider it their permanent dwelling. They belong to their new family permanently.

So with us – we have been adopted. We belong to our new family. However, if our sense of fellowship with Father God has dulled and we do not feel as though we are part of this family, we might be tempted to downplay this truth. Yet the basis of adoption is that whatever we feel, the adoption still stands.

Our adoption has been decreed by God and if we ever doubt it, the words in today's passage serve as our adoption papers to which we can return to check the validity of our new status. A good way of feeding the truth about our adoption is to worship Father God for what he has done, whether we feel it or not, because it has been revealed to us in the Bible.

You may like to repeat these words to yourself for a few minutes: 'I belong to the Father.' Remember it is not about your feelings, but about the truth revealed to us in the New Testament. Begin to thank him for adopting you and wanting you to be part of his family.

JOHN RYELAND

24/7 action

But when the fullness of time had come, God sent his Son, born of a woman, born under the law, in order to redeem those who were under the law, so that we might receive adoption as children. And because you are children, God has sent the Spirit of his Son into our hearts, crying, 'Abba! Father!' So you are no longer a slave but a child, and if a child then also an heir through God.

Paul's words in this passage give us great hope and encouragement in our attempts to comprehend God as Father, particularly those of us who might have been struggling with this concept because of negative experiences of fatherhood in our own lives. The reason for this hope is that these words assure us that recognising God as our loving Father has nothing to do with us trying to change our mindset or grasping new truths that feel contrary to our past experiences. Instead, we are told that there is something going on within us, even when we are totally unaware of it, that is beyond our control. It is this: God has put the Spirit of his Son, Jesus, into our hearts to actively grow this concept of God's intimate fatherhood within each of us.

We read that the Spirit is within us, calling out, 'Abba! Father!' (v. 6). Presumably this is not for his benefit, since he is already in a glorious relationship with God, so it must be for our good! He is calling out these words within us so that we might absorb them in the deepest part of our being and be transformed. I love the fact that this is an activity going on within us, regardless of whether we feel it. The Father is growing intimacy within us, whatever our experience might have been.

One obvious response to this should be to offer worship as a genuine act of thankfulness to God.

As you sit quietly, try saying 'Abba' to yourself as you breathe in and 'Father' as you breathe out. Try to catch the wonder and the truth that what you are doing is reflecting the continuous action of the Holy Spirit.

JOHN RYELAND

59

Taking a broader view

Then God said, 'Let us make humans in our image, according to our likeness, and let them have dominion over the fish of the sea and over the birds of the air and over the cattle and over all the wild animals of the earth and over every creeping thing that creeps upon the earth.' So God created humans in his image, in the image of God he created them; male and female he created them.

Father is one aspect of God expressed in the Trinity, along with Son and Holy Spirit. Generally most people are happy to accept this expression of the godhead, but there are those who would also like to see the notion of motherhood expressed in the Trinity. For some this might be contentious, raising questions about whether this portrayal is biblical. Today's verses address this.

At the start of the book of Genesis, right at the beginning of the Bible, there is the suggestion of the fullness of God being both male and female. It is the creation of humankind as male and female that is an expression of the likeness of God. This suggests to me that the concept of the fatherhood of God is not something that we can fully equate with gender roles. We could try to list what we think of as paternal roles and maternal roles in parenting, but such a list is bound to reflect our own cultural expectations and personal experiences.

While it is true that the Spirit is inwardly forming and encouraging our personal understanding of the fatherhood of God, it may well be that aspects of parenting more traditionally recognised as maternal qualities are equally applicable to him. So rather than trying to identify the differences between father and mother figures, thereby drawing a distinction between them, it might be helpful to embrace all these qualities to glimpse a fuller picture of God as our Father.

As you worship Father God for all he has done for you, seek to expand your perception of who he is by pondering the positive influences of both your father and your mother, as well as others who have positively influenced you. Let this feed your worship of the greatness of God.

JOHN RYELAND

Being in a right relationship

For as the heavens are high above the earth, so great is his steadfast love towards those who fear him; as far as the east is from the west, so far he removes our transgressions from us. As a father has compassion for his children, so the Lord has compassion for those who fear him. For he knows how we were made; he remembers that we are dust.

Compassion and fear sound like an odd combination! If fear is a prerequisite for compassion, it creates the strange notion that God's compassion is dependent on an appropriate emotion in us. However, the Hebrew word for fear can encompass a variety of meanings that are not conveyed by our word. One of these is the right relation of children to their parents, which is probably better translated as honour or respect.

This does not mean that we should worry in case we are not honouring God sufficiently; it is more about the state of our hearts. Of course there are ways that we could do better, but generally we are seeking to discover more about the reality of God as Father and to give more of our lives to him. The relationship is that of a father and his children, not a judge in a courtroom!

Nor does this passage mean that the Lord only has compassion on those who honour him. Most parents have a special place in their hearts for their own children, but this does not mean that they are incapable of having compassion for many other people as well. In the same way, God's love is for everyone, but as his children who are seeking to work out our relationship with him, we have a special place in his heart.

Today's passage calls us back to a vision of God as the Father of compassion, so let us endeavour to keep revisiting this beautiful description of him and recognise his utter delight in us.

Take a few moments to consider the parent who loves and delights in their children, and then translate it to the delight that Father God has in you. However imperfect you may feel, his delight is in you as his child. What difference will this make to you today?

JOHN RYELAND

Being still and content

O Lord, my heart is not lifted up; my eyes are not raised too high; I do not occupy myself with things too great and too marvellous for me. But I have calmed and quieted my soul, like a weaned child with its mother; my soul is like the weaned child that is with me. O Israel, hope in the Lord from this time on and forevermore.

This beautiful picture is not so much about God's parenthood but more about us as his children. The picture of the weaned child with his or her mother is very powerful. It is not an image of a child desperately seeking food from its mother or crying for an unmet need; rather, it is a picture of a child who has had their fill and is happy to rest with its mother, simply for the joy of being there. The child still has needs, of course, but while seeking to have those needs met there is pleasure and contentment in the relationship. This is the state that the writer of today's psalm has worked to achieve, and it presents us with a challenge to do likewise.

I am certainly not suggesting that it is wrong to bring our needs to God. When we do so we are exercising faith and trust in him as our provider, as well as being obedient to the command in 1 Peter 5:7: 'Cast all your anxiety on him, because he cares for you.' However, if that is all we do when we pray and our prayer requests form the totality of our prayer lives, we are missing out on the picture that this psalm so graphically shares with us. Prayer is also about resting and being still with God.

We do not need to do or say anything in particular at these times; it is just a matter of making the space in our lives to simply be with God and know we are together.

---

*When you have brought all your requests to God,
rather than rushing off, sit in the quiet knowing that he is still there.
You do not have to say anything or expect anything to happen –
simply be there, knowing that he is there too.*

JOHN RYELAND

Being willing

'Jerusalem, Jerusalem, the city that kills the prophets and stones those who are sent to it! How often have I desired to gather your children together as a hen gathers her brood under her wings, and you were not willing! See, your house is left to you, desolate. For I tell you, you will not see me again until you say, "Blessed is the one who comes in the name of the Lord."'

We have been exploring the concept of Father God, and his parenthood. This verse gives us a glimpse of it from God's perspective. Today's words were spoken by Jesus, not as a threat of judgement, but rather to express a profound sadness that God was being deprived of the love he so longed to pour out upon his children.

The words were spoken over Jerusalem, but the personal nature of the language suggests that Jesus' message was directed to the individuals living there, rather than to the bricks and mortar that formed the city itself. The inhabitants were 'the brood' who needed the love of their mother – but sadly were not willing.

The challenge for us is whether we are willing to receive and rest in God's love? This involves commitment to spending the time and making the effort to cast aside any feelings that may cause us to doubt his love and to actively pursue the truth of the love relationship between him and us.

The effect of us doing this is not simply a selfish attempt to feel more loved, but rather so that we can embrace the things dear to God's heart and not reject them, as he felt the city of Jerusalem had done. By embracing his purposes, the effect of his love upon us will overflow to an expression of his love towards others.

The call to receive Father God's love is a deep challenge to us all. Are you willing to receive this love and to let it change you?

How hard has it been to believe in Father God's love for you?
What has been the hardest part and the most difficult challenge?
As we have been seeking to focus on this love over the past two weeks,
have you sensed any change in your life with God?

JOHN RYELAND

Joseph's story

 Joseph's story is one we may feel we are already familiar with. It was one I learnt as a child – possibly encouraged by the musical *Joseph and the Amazing Technicolour Dreamcoat*, which is still popular and often staged today. But the story – found in the final chapters of Genesis – deserves revisiting. Its position at the end of that great narrative of relationship with God is about loss and uneasy regain. There is movement from the homeland of Abraham and the patriarchs to a new life in Egypt.

Joseph is an ambiguous character and not easy to like at first, being highly undiplomatic, although we are assured that he is blessed. His story addresses family relationships, reputation and social justice. It is also about forgiveness, the presence of God and opening up to new worlds.

Dreams feature to a greater or lesser degree. Can we look into the future? If we can, what good does that do us? Can we be open to our inner world? To God's voice? To those refugees at our borders? Throughout these readings we are reminded of God's promise for his people, but we also learn that the promise isn't exclusive. Blessing stretches out into other lands in spite of, or perhaps because of, the ravages of famine.

Joseph is a very different man at the end of these chapters than he was at the beginning – he is changed by the events that befall him. We can compare Joseph with Jesus, remembering that these are far earlier times and different philosophies. Themes of suffering, blessedness, reconciliation and forgiveness are common to both Joseph and Jesus, and it is interesting to note the similarities and differences.

Genesis is no modern novel. There is no explicit analysis of the characters' motivations, no stream-of-consciousness insight into Joseph's thoughts. Yet the story does not contain two-dimensional characters. What has impressed me about Joseph is how engrossing his character becomes. Like all the patriarchs, and even ourselves, he is no plaster saint. His character is compromised, like David, Solomon and the disciples. But somehow or other he is blessed. Let us find out what that means for him.

HARRY SMART

What sort of coat?

Joseph, being seventeen years old, was shepherding the flock with his brothers; he was a helper to the sons of Bilhah and Zilpah, his father's wives, and Joseph brought a bad report of them to their father. Now Israel loved Joseph more than any other of his children because he was the son of his old age, and he made him an ornamented robe. But when his brothers saw that their father loved him more than all his brothers, they hated him and could not speak peaceably to him.

Jacob, also known as Israel, one of Isaac's twin sons, was born clutching his brother Esau's heel (Genesis 25:26) and had an issue with position in the family. His deception of his father Isaac to obtain his blessing led to a series of incidents that lead him to God's presence and promises.

Jacob is a bit of a hero for me – he is quite wily, and he struggles with God, with whom he seems to be on a rather tortuous journey. He is rather ambiguous, like the most interesting heroes. He has dreams too. Being old now, he should perhaps be wiser, but his flaws run through the story of his son Joseph. He passes on his biased love, clearly preferring Joseph. Does Joseph make an elderly father feel young? Is it because he was the younger brother himself?

Counselling training stresses the importance of where you are in the family. I am an only child, which is like being the eldest and youngest. You have to do things first, but also be the youngest. There is no one to copy, and no one to follow you. These relationships are key, and Jacob is certainly no better than most in his fathering skills.

Jacob sets Joseph up for trouble with the gift of the 'ornamented robe' – entirely impractical for hard labour as a shepherd. Older translations famously described it as of many colours. Joseph has already passed on bad reports to his father about his father's wives. Furthermore, as if to add insult to injury, he seems to delight in reporting his dreams of his superiority to his brothers, as we will see tomorrow.

How do we balance prophecy and tact?

HARRY SMART

Any dream?

Once Joseph had a dream, and when he told it to his brothers, they hated him even more. He said to them, 'Listen to this dream that I dreamed. There we were, binding sheaves in the field. Suddenly my sheaf rose and stood upright; then your sheaves gathered round it and bowed down to my sheaf.' His brothers said to him, 'Are you indeed to reign over us? Are you indeed to have dominion over us?' So they hated him even more because of his dreams and his words. He had another dream, and told it to his brothers saying, 'Look, I have had another dream: the sun, the moon, and eleven stars were bowing down to me.'

Some people do not know when to stop. Joseph is certainly no diplomat! Later, Joseph interprets other people's dreams in Egypt. His father Jacob had a dream not to be afraid of leaving the promised land. He had also dreamt of the angels' ladder up to heaven. Has Jacob stopped dreaming? Perhaps he has learnt tact in the meantime.

Should Joseph have kept his dream to himself? If we view them as predictions of his power and superiority over his family, then they are very relevant to his life – he will come to have almost ultimate power over them when they plea for food, and in the tests he sets them. The dreams spur on his brothers' anger – if he had kept quiet, they might not have contemplated murdering him. The baker and the steward would have met their fates with or without warning. The response to Pharaoh's dream of great harvest and of starvation would have been different without Joseph's interpretation.

I have been privileged to meet some geniuses, among them a psychiatrist who was a good friend and who died several years ago. He was able to make people feel interesting and worthwhile, when he could have made us feel slow and dull. Knowledge and power can either build up or disempower and destroy. The older Joseph is more aware of the damaging potential of power, but the boy Joseph does not know what to do with his superpowers just yet.

What is your superpower? How do you use it and to what effect?

HARRY SMART

Being thankful

Now Joseph was taken down to Egypt, and Potiphar, an officer of Pharaoh, the captain of the guard, an Egyptian, bought him from the Ishmaelites who had brought him down there. The Lord was with Joseph, and he became a successful man; he was in the house of his Egyptian master. His master saw that the Lord was with him and that the Lord caused all that he did to prosper in his hands.

Joseph's story confronts us with ideas of blessing and success. Sold into slavery by his own family, he is now in a foreign country, someone else's possession. Yet he is described as blessed. Being discovered by the Midianites and sold in Egypt opens up a new world for him.

I regularly lead mindfulness retreats for NHS staff. We talk about living in an 'attitude of gratitude'. Being thankful and seeing the good in situations is less stressful and a healthier way of living. It is one I struggle with. I can come up with a list of problems, get caught in my own worries. I need to remember or be reminded of the good things – which is why I enjoy stopping on a walk on a spring day and hearing the birds. I feel myself opening up as I concentrate on the world outside myself.

I remember car stickers which read 'If you can read this, thank a teacher'. We will all have people that we can thank: teachers, certainly (thank you, Mr Gaskin), as well as parents, friends, strangers. Thank you to the people who serviced my car today – I could not do it – but thank you also to those I find difficult – I have learnt from you too, and sometimes grown more too.

Sometimes blessings are also challenges. If I have enough to eat today, others may not. If I live in peace, I know that others are dying in war today. These may come at the expense of others, so perhaps they are not blessings at all.

It is fine to be successful, to be good at one's job. I had a work review a little while ago. The review went well and was encouraging. It is good to praise others and also to accept praise as well.

What have you got to be thankful for today?

HARRY SMART

Out of the depths

When his master heard the words that his wife spoke to him, saying, 'This is the way your servant treated me,' he became enraged. And Joseph's master took him and put him into the prison, the place where the king's prisoners were confined; he remained there in prison. But the Lord was with Joseph and showed his steadfast love; he gave him favour in the sight of the chief jailer.

There are not many women in Joseph's story, and we only know Potiphar's wife in relation to her husband. She unsuccessfully plays the role of temptress. Joseph is in a world of extreme power, very different from that displayed by Jacob and his family. Potiphar owns slaves, and Pharaoh orders executions. Potiphar's wife is also used to getting what she wants. She sees something attractive about him. We are given a general physical description of Joseph, and perhaps she is responding to his character as well, the sense that he is blessed by God.

Those who live in a world where they can possess what they want can be corrupted by their wealth. Where our relationships become commercialised, where we cannot recognise the integrity of the other, we dishonour ourselves as well as them. Even as Potiphar is casting Joseph into prison, we are reminded that God was with him. Perhaps Potiphar suspected that Joseph was not really guilty, which is why he was not treated more cruelly. Joseph is shown steadfast love by God – he is better treated than he might have expected and is still alive to find favour in the eyes of the chief jailer.

Nelson Mandela endured and survived imprisonment in South Africa. He behaved with dignity and courage but suffered isolation and beating. He gained the respect of his fellow prisoners and also his captors. One visitor said he set the pace at which his prison guards escorted him. He learnt Afrikaans, intending to discover the attitudes of those he opposed, but it also helped him to respond with greater understanding of the Afrikaans community. Without his greatness of spirit during captivity, South Africa might have been more riven by unrest and civil war than it was.

Matthew 25 encourages us to visit prisoners.
What is the church's ministry in that context?

HARRY SMART

I shall walk at liberty

Then Pharaoh sent for Joseph, and he was hurriedly brought out of the dungeon. When he had shaved himself and changed his clothes, he came in before Pharaoh. And Pharaoh said to Joseph, 'I had a dream, and there is no one who can interpret it. I have heard it said of you that when you hear a dream you can interpret it.' Joseph answered Pharaoh, 'It is not I; God will give Pharaoh a favourable answer.'

Joseph may be blessed, but his fate seems to be at the whim of those more powerful than him: the chief cupbearer, who forgets his promise to plead his case until the royal dreams occur, and Pharaoh, who interviews the once-forgotten prisoner. Any interview guide will recommend that when you are about to meet the leader of a world power, you should make yourself presentable, and that is what Joseph does.

Joseph promises Pharaoh favourable answers, but his interpretation of the dreams is only partly so. As with his previous elucidations, Joseph does not shy away from bad news. Could he have withheld the meaning of the threatening lean cows with 'let's emphasise the positive'? Politicians have hidden behind vague explanations before when the truth seems too hard.

Pharaoh will have heard sycophancy before and would not be impressed. The urgency of Joseph's warning strikes him; he recognises a clear vision and the need to respond. Joseph can be excused from almost proposing himself as the best man for the job of 'a discerning and wise' manager.

Joseph warns of grievous times beyond the first seven years of plenty. Egypt was a superpower for millennia, sustained by the Nile trade routes and its ancient civilisation. Protected from serious famine, it is complacent about its potential to survive shortages. The dreams are shocking: cows and grain consumed by want and starvation. Soon the famine will bring refugees in search of sustenance and support.

Many within and beyond the church have warned of climate change, and the damage to our environment, unjust trade and our responsibilities as part of creation made in the image of our creator.

---

*How can we convey the urgency of environmental concern
in our worship and daily lives?*

HARRY SMART

Seeing blessing

He gathered up all the food of the seven years when there was plenty in the land of Egypt and stored up food in the cities; he stored up in every city the food from the fields around it. So Joseph stored up grain in such abundance – like the sand of the sea—that he stopped measuring it; it was beyond measure.

The theme of blessing flows throughout Genesis, which is noteworthy considering that we mostly associate the book with the fall, the most profound loss of God's favour and close relationship. Joseph is blessed. He does not live a charmed existence – bad things happen to him all the time – but he is blessed in his determination to keep getting up when he has been knocked down. He does not succumb to despair. His blessing is recognised by Potiphar and by Pharaoh, but not by most of his family, at least at first.

The language describing the grain as 'like the sands of the sea' recalls the blessing made to Abraham about how numerous his offspring would be (Genesis 22:17). The Egyptians are partaking in that blessing and Joseph is the conduit.

What is a blessing? I have in my time blessed benches, wedding rings and water for baptism. I have blessed marriages and the dying. In those cases it is a declaration of what is good – the bench will provide rest, the marriage may be a good one, the death will be peaceful and lead to new life. Sometimes I am blessing something that already seems sacred – a dying person, a congregation, a patient. But a blessing is also practical. In Luke 6:21, the hungry are declared blessed 'for you will be filled'.

When harvest fails, the hunger begins. Our food supply systems are still vulnerable – due to poor weather and complicated trading we have had shortages recently. Rising food prices bring hardship. In Egypt harvest meant life or death for many. We know the damage being done to our environment and species extinctions and we have had many warnings about the future. How are we preparing ourselves?

Joseph interprets the dreams through God's blessing and plans ahead. People come from afar for bread and Pharaoh welcomes them.

What does blessing mean for you? Can it be practical?

HARRY SMART

Crossing the border

When Jacob learned that there was grain in Egypt, he said to his sons, 'Why do you keep looking at one another? I have heard,' he said, 'that there is grain in Egypt; go down and buy grain for us there, that we may live and not die.' So ten of Joseph's brothers went down to buy grain in Egypt. But Jacob did not send Joseph's brother Benjamin with his brothers, for he feared that harm might come to him.

All the world has come to Egypt for grain and bread because of the preparation that Joseph has put into action, and Jacob sends his sons to join the many others buying grain. From his tone it seems that the sons are rather difficult to motivate. Jacob is making it clear how grave the situation has become – 'that we may live and not die' (v. 2).

Displaced peoples need places of welcome, countries that will open their borders, now as well as then. For those who have offered accommodation to Ukrainian refugees new contacts will have been made and experiences had that will leave profound effects. Jacob is having to think outside of his home territory – Egypt is a very different culture to his own nomadic one, and to his personal and familial relationship with God. Jacob decides not to send his youngest brother Benjamin. Again favouritism plays a part in the drama.

Joseph recognises his brothers, and he remembers his dreams (vv. 7–9) – is this an opportunity to enjoy his power over them? They had plotted to kill him after all, but he is toying with them and, although the brothers are an unsympathetic bunch, their plight and his almost supernatural knowledge of them do lead me to pity them. He demands to see their youngest brother, knowing this will hurt Jacob and frighten them. Perhaps he enjoys the sound of the jail door slamming closed.

The desire for revenge is difficult to acknowledge. Revenge is one of the impulses which is most commonly related in films – think of how many involve it as a motivation. Do we just want to get our own back? One of the significant elements of the crucifixion is that revenge's cycle was broken.

Can we recognise the desire for revenge but not act on it?

Does Christ's example help us move beyond revenge?

HARRY SMART

You reap what you sow

On the third day Joseph said to them, 'Do this and you will live, for I fear God: if you are honest men, let one of your brothers stay here where you are imprisoned… They said to one another, 'Alas, we are paying the penalty for what we did to our brother; we saw his anguish when he pleaded with us, but we would not listen. This is why anguish has come upon us.'

The final chapters of Genesis change approach somewhat from the beginning of Joseph's story. We are entering into an examination of guilt, expiation and forgiveness.

The brothers are only now beginning to feel guilty about how they have treated Joseph. They have not recognised him, but something is awakening these feelings. They feel they are being punished for how they treated him, but do not know how things are interconnected. Now their father's remaining favourite son is being demanded by the Egyptian vizier. 'Do this and you will live,' says Joseph (v. 18). Already they have faced potential death through starvation; now he is threatening them with death if they do not obey him.

Their sense of guilt is a start; they need to recognise that what they did was wrong. But they do not know how to correct the situation, and they are afraid of repercussions they do not yet understand. I have known patients who have felt incredibly guilty for things or feelings that they have had – anger, desire or resentment. People with mental health problems may struggle with feelings that plague them or which they feel are unacceptable. Guilt can mark where something has gone wrong, but sometimes it is imposed by others and becomes destructive – in cases of abuse, for example, where the abused person has been told it is their fault.

Ultimately this needs to be addressed – is it reasonable? Guilt which leaves us powerless is damaging. Imagine if Joseph had not eventually revealed himself to his brothers. Doing so releases such potential for regrowth and new relationship. This reminds us of the saving actions of Christ and of our relationship with our loving creator, mirrored in these final passages of Genesis.

Is guilt good or bad? Where does our moral sense come from?

HARRY SMART

Bereavement

'Take double the money with you. Carry back with you the money that was returned in the top of your sacks; perhaps it was an oversight. Take your brother also, and be on your way again to the man; may God Almighty grant you mercy before the man, so that he may send back your other brother and Benjamin. As for me, if I am bereaved of my children, I am bereaved.'

Jacob does not want to lose Benjamin, Joseph's brother by Rachel, who Jacob loved most. He faces such great loss that he fears he will be defined by his mourning.

It is wrong for a parent to face the prospect of the death of their child. Jacob is handing Benjamin over into a situation where he is in jeopardy. Letting go of a child to university, a new partner, a new town or country is risky in itself. But death rips its way through so much. The world is turned upside down.

Clients of mine have described themselves as always at the graveside – there is nowhere else they can be in their thoughts. Friends may advise the bereaved to 'get over it', to move on and learn to live again. In their own time the person does need to move away from the graveside, integrate the loss into their lives, honouring what has happened but also recognise their own right to meaningful life.

Jacob continues to favour Benjamin. He is anxious for his young son being sent to Joseph but shows no concern for the son who has been left behind in Egypt as surety. Jacob cannot see what he is doing. His marriage to Rachel and her death have trapped him in behaviour that does more harm than good. Rachel's resentment at being unable to bear children, her father's trickery in marrying her older sister to Jacob first, are added to the mix that continues to poison the family. Genesis begins with Adam and Eve's expulsion from paradise. From there it continues to plot how blessing and harm are passed across from generation to generation.

Joseph could continue the harm through his manipulation of his brothers, but he is moved to tears at the sight of Benjamin and news of his father.

If you have experienced loss, what has helped you to begin to recover?

HARRY SMART

To preserve life

Then Joseph said to his brothers, 'Come closer to me.' And they came closer. He said, 'I am your brother, Joseph, whom you sold into Egypt. And now do not be distressed or angry with yourselves, because you sold me here, for God sent me before you to preserve life. For the famine has been in the land these two years, and there are five more years in which there will be neither ploughing nor harvest. God sent me before you to preserve for you a remnant on earth and to keep alive for you many survivors.'

Jacob has played a long game, testing and challenging his brothers, but it has been hard for him too. The arrogant young man has been revealed to have many layers: passive aggression, manipulativeness, generosity and forgiveness. He has secretly wept when hearing his brothers discuss their guilt. Now he is moved to reveal himself.

In one of the most open-hearted and moving passages in Genesis, he forgives them because 'God sent me before you to preserve life' (v. 5). This is not an easy forgiveness or rationalisation. It might not be credible if we had not seen his caution earlier. He has changed through his experiences, and his insight has not been easily won.

'Forgive us our sins, for we ourselves forgive' is key within the Christian faith, as expressed in the Lord's Prayer (Luke 11:2–4). I admire those who forgive people who have harmed them. A family story tells of how one of my German relatives and an American soldier, both badly wounded, supported one another to get to the closest hospital at the end of the war.

For Joseph, forgiveness is only part of the outworking of his rejection by his brothers. He has been enslaved, imprisoned and then freed to save his new country and his family from famine. It would be insensitive to say to Joseph while he was being sold into slavery, 'Don't worry, in the future it will all be worth it.' Holding ourselves and others in kindness and compassion, including those with whom we find it difficult to get on, can overcome boundaries. I lead an exercise in our retreats which looks at doing this, though I warn participants that it might be difficult.

Take a breath and allow yourself to be aware
of God's forgiveness and presence.

HARRY SMART

The cost of everything

'There is nothing left in the sight of my lord but our bodies and our lands. Shall we die before your eyes, both we and our land? Buy us and our land in exchange for food. We with our land will become slaves to Pharaoh; just give us seed, so that we may live and not die and that the land may not become desolate.' So Joseph bought all the land of Egypt for Pharaoh. All the Egyptians sold their fields, because the famine was severe upon them, and the land became Pharaoh's.

If in the saga of Joseph's family reconciliation we had forgotten the seriousness of external events, we are reminded now. That haunting phrase 'so that we may live and not die' recurs. Joseph could have had his brothers killed when he set them up with the coins in their bags, or decided that they were spies checking Egypt's weaknesses. Meanwhile Egypt faces famine.

Jacob has risked leaving his home. The brothers have developed a conscience. With power over life and death, Joseph holds back. His own suffering has led him to be able to sustain the life of others – the people of his new adopted country and his fellow Canaanites. That is the great expression of his faith and of his blessing and which makes him exceptional.

The Egyptians' plight has led them to sell their land and become slaves to Pharaoh, and Joseph accepts the offer. Slavery was very common in the ancient world. Is Joseph abusing his power? Even if he has to make money from selling the grain and has to administer its distribution, buying people's lives is abhorrent. Are we left with the sense that a good man can nonetheless be exploitative and corrupt? Nowadays, big business managers can sometimes be divorced from their public responsibilities, though they may be 'good' people. Perhaps this is simply an attempt to explain land ownership in Egypt as the narrator understood it. These events took place possibly 1,500 years before Christ, and society has changed considerably. Yet my sense of discomfort remains.

---

*How do we cope with the inconsistencies within others
and within ourselves? Should there be a divide
between personal and public in our lives?*

HARRY SMART

Take me home

When the time of Israel's death drew near, he called his son Joseph and said to him, 'If I have found favour with you, put your hand under my thigh and promise to deal loyally and truly with me. Do not bury me in Egypt. When I lie down with my ancestors, carry me out of Egypt and bury me in their burial place.' He answered, 'I will do as you have said.' And he said, 'Swear to me,' and he swore to him. Then Israel bowed himself on the head of his bed.

My dad had a map of South Uist in the Outer Hebrides on his desk. We had often visited when I was a teenager, and my parents went on several occasions since then. He loved the islands and dreamt of living there, but he did not go back as often as he would have liked. Before he died, he reminded me of the map and indicated where he wanted his ashes to be scattered.

An eventful car journey and bad weather meant his ashes were scattered in a river, in what is perhaps the most beautiful landscape in the British Isles. It was not quite a homecoming, rather a reuniting with a place he deeply loved with family significance. My love for the islands and for Scotland continues, expressed partly in a passion for Harris tweed!

Jacob lays out his plans for his burial. He has been welcomed to Egypt, but it is not his home, and he wants to return to his ancestors' land. Home is another country; he is an exile. Sometimes we might feel like exiles, perhaps like my father, away from somewhere we love or in a country we no longer feel we belong to. Augustine prayed: 'Our hearts are restless till they find their rest in you.' We can feel detached, disconnected from our creator.

Dying Matters is a movement that encourages people to think about what they want when they die: care in the last days of life, wills and funeral plans, for example. I think of the Macmillan nurses who helped a patient be wheeled into the courtyard to feel the breeze when he was dying. It was his final wish.

It may be uncomfortable, but have you discussed what you want for the last days of your life?

HARRY SMART

What's in a name?

When Israel saw Joseph's sons, he said, 'Who are these?' Joseph said to his father, 'They are my sons, whom God has given me here.' And he said, 'Bring them to me, please, that I may bless them.' Now the eyes of Israel were dim with age, and he could not see well. So Joseph brought them near him; and he kissed them and embraced them.

Pharaoh gave Joseph a wife, Asenath, daughter of Potiphera, a priest. Commentators have suggested this might be the same Potiphar. They have two children with unusual but significant names: Manasseh, 'God made me forget all my hardship and all my father's house', and Ephraim, 'For God has made me fruitful in the land of my misfortunes' (Genesis 41:50–52).

Names have meanings. Alfred means 'elf counsel', Kylie means 'boomerang' and Noah means 'rest'. Introducing his two children to Jacob must have been awkward for Joseph. He has found himself a home in Egypt. His wife Asenath is an Egyptian aristocrat, whose name means 'belonging to Neith', a goddess. He has settled into the culture and practices of Egypt, though his faith in God continues to be real, as we see when he speaks with his brothers.

Does Jacob know what his sons did to Joseph? He welcomes his new grandsons and asks to bless them so that they may share in the promises made to him by God. Jacob wants to put right what has happened. He includes his lost son's family in his blessing.

All families have secrets. Sometimes they need addressing: abuse, for example, or selling your brother into slavery. Such secrets can continue to harm for generations. Sometimes it may be best to let stories fade or disappear. Returning soldiers rarely speak about what they have seen or done. I remember one elderly gentleman who simply said to me, 'Some bad things happened in that war.' I got little more from him, but somehow he was confessing to me when he knew that his remaining time was limited. It was enough to indicate recognition that he had been involved in something he regretted.

How easy is it to start a new page? When should we let go of the past?

HARRY SMART

To preserve a numerous people

So they approached Joseph, saying, 'Your father gave this instruction before he died, "Say to Joseph: I beg you, forgive the crime of your brothers and the wrong they did in harming you." Now therefore please forgive the crime of the servants of the God of your father.' Joseph wept when they spoke to him. Then his brothers also wept… But Joseph said to them, 'Do not be afraid! Am I in the place of God? Even though you intended to do harm to me, God intended it for good, in order to preserve a numerous people, as he is doing today. So have no fear; I myself will provide for you and your little ones.'

This is a long, but key passage in Joseph's story. Do we believe his brothers? Without the protection of their father, they feel vulnerable to Joseph's vengeance. Did Jacob know what Joseph's brothers did to him? Joseph has enough power to have them put to death or at least to be exiled if he wants. Jacob's wishes, even if genuine, could only appeal to his better nature.

Yet Joseph has attained a freedom from the sufferings that have befallen him. He is not defined by his brokenness or by his brothers' treatment of him. His brothers do not seem to recognise that he is independent of them – he has the freedom to choose to be merciful, they cannot threaten him with his father's last wishes into letting them live.

That freedom comes through self-knowledge and, for Joseph (and for us too), through trust in God. He has not been free from resentment; he plays games with them when they are dependent upon him. But he is also blessed.

Perhaps we come to a closer understanding of what being blessed means in this context. Joseph is not defined by his hurt. He has felt anger, but he can forgive. He knows that he is not God, the reference point of all life, even though he is very powerful. He weeps in his own pain, but also feels the pain of those who have hurt him.

Getting to know Joseph's story has led me to a real admiration of him and recognition of why his story is important and relevant today. What has stood out for you from Joseph's story?

HARRY SMART

Titus and Philemon

 Picture a man walking from place to place on a Greek island. He is not on holiday; he has a job to do, visiting Christian groups in the various communities on Crete to remind them of the basics of the gospel and its implications for daily life. He also needs to appoint local leaders in each place, and where he finds unhelpful teaching, to try to stamp it out. He has a timescale of a few months at most, then he must move on.

He carries with him a letter from his mentor, reminding him of what he must do and teach. While it is addressed personally to him, the letter is not intended for his reading alone. Where people dislike his approach or have different priorities from his, he can use his mentor's instructions as his authority. Many of the people he meets know and respect that older teacher, and they are certainly more likely to take note of what *he* says. The mentor's name was Paul; the traveller is Titus. We will dig into the letter he carries over the next few days.

Now picture a second man, walking through what today is western Turkey. He is rather anxious: the end of this journey may prove awkward or even dangerous for him. He is not alone, though. He has companions who are older in the Christian faith than he is; and some of them know Philemon, the man they are going to see. A comparison of names in Philemon 1–2, 23–25 with Colossians 4:7–17 indicates Colossae as their probable destination.

These travellers are also carrying a letter from Paul. This one, addressed to his friend Philemon, pleads for the anxious man (named Onesimus) to be given a second chance. Onesimus is a runaway slave, returning to Philemon, his master, with no legal rights whatsoever. But he has recently embraced the same faith as Philemon. This, Paul argues, puts their relationship on a new footing. As the person who brought Philemon to faith in Christ, Paul says Philemon should treat Onesimus with Christian kindness. Onesimus certainly hopes he will!

Both these letters are quite short. Why not read each of them in full before we look at what they say to us?

MARTIN LECKEBUSCH

Leaders needed

The reason I left you in Crete was that you might put in order what was left unfinished and appoint elders in every town, as I directed you. An elder must be blameless, faithful to his wife, a man whose children believe and are not open to the charge of being wild and disobedient. Since an overseer manages God's household, he must be blameless – not overbearing, not quick-tempered, not given to drunkenness, not violent, not pursuing dishonest gain. Rather, he must be hospitable, one who loves what is good, who is self-controlled, upright, holy and disciplined. He must hold firmly to the trustworthy message as it has been taught, so that he can encourage others by sound doctrine and refute those who oppose it.

Some of the groups Titus was to visit were probably quite small; they could have been largely made up of people who had only recently begun their Christian journey. These folk would have had a real experience of God, beginning from when Paul and his companions travelled through the island and announced the news about Jesus. However, many of them probably had no real grasp of the Old Testament scriptures which foretold Jesus' coming nor the details of Jesus' teaching and miracles. They were enthusiastic for their new faith and probably keen to share it, but how? What next?

These groups needed leadership. Titus' job was to identify the emerging leaders and to point them – and hence their fledgling congregations – in the right direction. Interestingly, Paul's criteria say nothing about academic qualifications and surprisingly little about gifts. The key focus is character, shown in daily living. Self-restraint is one of his essential tests. He is looking for people who have won the respect of their children – where is consistency harder than at home? Yet they must also be able to explain and defend the faith. In short, by their words but especially by their lives they are to be good examples to other believers and good advertisements of the message to outsiders.

Lord Jesus, may all those with leadership roles and responsibilities in your church have the stability and integrity of character you alone can provide. And may that be true for me, as well. Amen.

MARTIN LECKEBUSCH

The challenge of culture

For there are many rebellious people, full of meaningless talk and deception, especially those of the circumcision group. They must be silenced, because they are disrupting whole households by teaching things they ought not to teach – and that for the sake of dishonest gain. One of Crete's own prophets has said it: 'Cretans are always liars, evil brutes, lazy gluttons.' This saying is true. Therefore rebuke them sharply, so that they will be sound in the faith… To the pure, all things are pure, but to those who are corrupted and do not believe, nothing is pure. In fact, both their minds and consciences are corrupted. They claim to know God, but by their actions they deny him. They are detestable, disobedient and unfit for doing anything good.

I once heard a preacher ask: 'Who'd be a Cretan?' Paul certainly has little positive to say about the island's inhabitants. The description he quotes here (with approval!) may help explain why self-control was one of his crucial benchmarks for church leaders. He also warns Titus here and elsewhere about people whose approach to the existing scriptures (our Old Testament) was heavily influenced by obscure, controversial ideas which did nothing to encourage godly living.

Yet every culture has its flaws and biases, and we all unconsciously absorb the values, good and bad, of the people among whom we live, especially as we grow up. The result is that when we come to Christ, we may have plenty to unlearn if we are truly to become who he wants us to be, which is to be like him. We may not want to think we ever had corrupt consciences or were unfit for doing anything good, but what, without God's grace, are we?

Perhaps the greatest challenge in these verses is the practical test of daily conduct which Paul implicitly sets out. If I claim to know God, do my actions undermine that claim? What do I need to unlearn?

'Examine yourselves to see whether you are in the faith; test yourselves. Do you not realise that Christ Jesus is in you – unless, of course, you fail the test?' (2 Corinthians 13:5). Help me, Lord Jesus, to live in a way that does not deny you. Amen.

MARTIN LECKEBUSCH

Truth modelled and applied

You, however, must teach what is appropriate to sound doctrine. Teach the older men to be temperate, worthy of respect, self-controlled, and sound in faith, in love and in endurance. Likewise, teach the older women to be reverent in the way they live, not to be slanderers or addicted to much wine, but to teach what is good. Then they can urge the younger women to love their husbands and children, to be self-controlled and pure, to be busy at home, to be kind, and to be subject to their husbands, so that no one will malign the word of God. Similarly, encourage the young men to be self-controlled. In everything set them an example by doing what is good.

Some Bible translations offer separate editions for women, men, youth and so on, with study notes added. Is that a good thing, or should we all read the same Bible text? What might the apostle Paul have thought? He is clear that when Titus instructs those new churches on Crete, his teaching must align with the core doctrines of the faith. That could have included the (Old Testament) scriptures, traditions about Jesus' life and teaching, and the insights which the apostles proclaimed (even if no one yet thought of these as 'new scriptures' when Paul wrote this). The central truths of the gospel were not negotiable – and still are not.

Conversely, Paul knew that the message would impact differently on various groups in the church, whose age and social position exposed them to different pressures, temptations, opportunities and responsibilities. He therefore urges Titus to tailor his application of the truth to his hearers' needs.

Several themes emerge. Self-control is mentioned repeatedly. Each group is to live in a way which models godliness for other people to see, whether as mentors within the church or to make their message appealing to outsiders. So Titus himself, presumably a comparatively young man, is to model what he teaches as well as instructing other people.

Authentic Christian living is countercultural. It does not demolish the social fabric, but it does present a better alternative.

May your Spirit guide me to apply the truth
as it is most needed in each part of my life. Amen.

MARTIN LECKEBUSCH

What does 'grace' mean?

For the grace of God has appeared that offers salvation to all people. It teaches us to say 'No' to ungodliness and worldly passions, and to live self-controlled, upright and godly lives in this present age, while we wait for the blessed hope – the appearing of the glory of our great God and Saviour, Jesus Christ, who gave himself for us to redeem us from all wickedness and to purify for himself a people that are his very own, eager to do what is good.

We should not overlook the significance of Paul's statement about salvation being offered to all people. Many of those who traced their ancestry to Abraham had come to believe quite firmly that God was really interested only in them, not in the other nations, despite their scriptures saying otherwise. Radically, though, the gospel opened the door to anyone who would respond. That is grace at work.

There is more: Christ gave himself to be our Saviour, even though he is God. Paul does not here explore the full mystery and wonder of Jesus' death and resurrection, but he does highlight two aspects of it. First, Jesus died to rescue us from wickedness: the consequences of our rebellion against God are removed as God declares us 'not guilty'. That, too, is grace. Second, complementing this, Jesus died to purify a people for himself. This involves changed attitudes: we respond gratefully to what Christ did by choosing to live differently. This is what Paul means by renouncing ungodliness to live upright lives from now on, enabled by God's Spirit. Once again, grace is at work.

There is nevertheless a tension here. We are not what we once were; nor yet are we what we should be and someday will be. Christian living strains forward, eagerly grasping the hope of God's promised future. Christ will return, taking his rightful place as King in the age which is yet to come – and finishing our transformation. Only then will the work of grace be complete.

We could summarise it like this: grace means God loves you just as you are, but he loves you too much to leave you like that.

Today, Lord, help me to respond to your grace
by living as you want me to. Amen.

MARTIN LECKEBUSCH

Saved to serve

At one time we too were foolish, disobedient, deceived and enslaved by all kinds of passions and pleasures. We lived in malice and envy, being hated and hating one another. But when the kindness and love of God our Saviour appeared, he saved us, not because of righteous things we had done, but because of his mercy. He saved us through the washing of rebirth and renewal by the Holy Spirit, whom he poured out on us generously through Jesus Christ our Saviour… I want you to stress these things, so that those who have trusted in God may be careful to devote themselves to doing what is good. These things are excellent and profitable for everyone.

It is not only the Cretans whom Paul thinks were once unpleasant – he applies his catalogue of vices here to himself as much as to anyone else. Yet Paul had undergone a tremendous change when God drew him to Christ. We saw earlier how graciously God deals with everyone who responds to the gospel; here, the emphasis is on the Holy Spirit, whose presence and power make that change real.

We would be mistaken to think that becoming a Christian involves merely agreeing with a checklist of beliefs. It should usher in a whole new way of living, reoriented by the hope of eternal life which God has given us as part of the package of being accepted in Christ.

Yet we would also be wrong if we thought of that new life as being mostly about our personal emotional satisfaction. Paul tells Titus to stress what he has written, so that these Christians will live differently, devoting themselves to doing good. Even more, that is not just for themselves and each other. True spirituality has an impact on all kinds of people around us and on the communities in which we live.

Once again, Paul's emphasis is upon lives which demonstrate God's way for living, making it appealing to outsiders. The apostle will not be satisfied until the believers' daily lives show the message of grace through practical action as well as in clear teaching.

Holy Spirit, may my life be faithful and fruitful, today and every day. Amen.

MARTIN LECKEBUSCH

Persuasion, or the prodigal servant

Your love has given me great joy and encouragement, because you, brother, have refreshed the hearts of the Lord's people. Therefore, although in Christ I could be bold and order you to do what you ought to do, yet I prefer to appeal to you on the basis of love. It is as none other than Paul – an old man and now also a prisoner of Christ Jesus – that I appeal to you for my son Onesimus, who became my son while I was in chains. Formerly he was useless to you, but now he has become useful both to you and to me.

What did Paul think as he wrote this letter? He was treading a delicate line. As outlined in the Introduction (see page 79), Onesimus was in a precarious position. Returning to his master was right, but difficult. The consequences may prove severe; he could legally be killed. Paul is understandably eager to prevent that.

Paul's approach is subtle. What he will ask is a bold demand, but it is tempered both by his gratitude for the faith of his dear friend Philemon and by some light wordplay. Onesimus means 'useful'; reshaped by his newfound faith, this formerly unproductive worker could at last live up to his name. More importantly, owner and slave are now also brothers in Christ.

Paul *almost* gives Philemon an order, but his persuasive pressure is gracious and friendly, not vindictive. He asks 'on the basis of love' (v. 9): his own affection for both Philemon and Onesimus; the grateful devotion Philemon feels towards him, and towards Christ; and Christ's unmeasured love for all three of them, Paul, Philemon and Onesimus.

Paul is clear: Philemon *should* forgive Onesimus as he, Philemon, has been forgiven by Christ. To do so would align with Philemon's good reputation as Christ's servant. The apostle even promises, later in the letter, to underwrite any debt between slave and master, putting that in the context of Philemon's own spiritual indebtedness.

This letter is a masterclass in how grace makes us rethink our reactions and see life differently.

'Blessed are the peacemakers' (Matthew 5:9). Pray for those who foster reconciliation, asking whether you could be among their number.

MARTIN LECKEBUSCH

The story of the unmerciful master?

I am sending him – who is my very heart – back to you. I would have liked to keep him with me so that he could take your place in helping me while I am in chains for the gospel. But I did not want to do anything without your consent, so that any favour you do would not seem forced but would be voluntary. Perhaps the reason he was separated from you for a little while was that you might have him back forever – no longer as a slave, but better than a slave, as a dear brother… So if you consider me a partner, welcome him as you would welcome me.

What did Philemon think as he read this letter? Here stood the runaway he had thought gone forever, and the scoundrel had met Philemon's father in Christ, who brought him, too, to faith. What should he do now? If he showed mercy, accepting Onesimus back, what message would that send to his other slaves? But if he refused, what would Paul say when he arrived? Philemon respected Paul greatly; now Paul wanted him to show that same attitude to this troublemaker who had caused him great inconvenience and, Philemon suspected, stolen from him as well. And if he did accept Onesimus back, then when the church met at Philemon's house, Onesimus should be sharing their meal together, not just preparing or serving it. What a conundrum!

Nothing definitively records what Philemon did. However, some traditions hint that Onesimus became bishop of Ephesus, while others say Philemon and Onesimus were both martyred during Nero's purges.

Why did Paul not insist that Philemon both welcome Onesimus and emancipate him? Why does the New Testament not argue explicitly against slavery? There are many possible reasons, especially given the vulnerability of the infant church in the Roman Empire. Nevertheless, the new basis of relationships between Christian slaves and slave-owners did eventually bear fruit in campaigns for slavery's abolition. Paul's letter to Philemon sowed some of the seeds which finally yielded that harvest.

Guide me, Lord, through life's demanding choices, to make good decisions whose benefits reach far beyond anything I can foresee. Amen.

MARTIN LECKEBUSCH

Holy days and holidays

I imagine that we have all had the experience of being on holiday and thinking, 'I wish everyday could be like this!' There is something unique and special about the experience of taking a holiday, whether that is an extended stay in some exotic clime, a couple of days away just a few miles down the road, or even a true 'staycation', time carved out at home which includes days out either locally or slightly further afield.

Many of us are aware that the word 'holiday' derives from 'holy day', those days in the church calendar set aside to mark key events in the Christian story – Christmas and Easter, for example – or special people, such as saints.

Despite the etymology, on the surface there is not much that is holy about the holidays we take nowadays. For many of us they feel like a luxury or an indulgence, something a little bit selfish that gives us a break from 'real life'. We may have saved for a long time to be able to afford a really special holiday, or we cherish an annual period set aside for quality time with friends or family.

Over the next two weeks we will consider whether there is more that is holy about our holidays than we might realise, and consider how we can bring that holiday holiness back into the pressures and ordinariness of everyday life.

You will see that each day's reading and reflection concludes not with a prayer, but with a suggestion for ways in which you might put that day's aspect of 'holiday' into practice. Some will 'just' need a little space and time on the day in question (I realise that in itself this will be a big ask for some); others will challenge you to take a practical action which might require some organisation and the wherewithal to spend some money. If you have a summer holiday planned, why not consider using these challenges while you take this time out?

Please do not feel obliged to complete these tasks; they are offered simply as an opportunity to think differently about how we navigate our way through each day. You may wish to simply pray that God will help you see the holy in the ordinary as you go through the day.

LOUISE DAVIS

Sabbath

'Remember the Sabbath day and keep it holy. Six days you shall labour and do all your work. But the seventh day is a Sabbath to the Lord your God; you shall not do any work – you, your son or your daughter, your male or female slave, your livestock, or the alien resident in your towns. For in six days the Lord made heaven and earth, the sea, and all that is in them, but rested the seventh day; therefore the Lord blessed the Sabbath day and consecrated it.'

As I started to think about holy days and holidays, the first idea I landed on was the concept of Sabbath and God's designation of it as a holy day. These verses from Exodus provide us with a helpful, concise definition of a holy day, which will keep us on track as we move through these next two weeks.

That said, while these verses give us a clear template for what the Sabbath day *should not* include – the work that enables you and your family to put food on the table and a roof over your head – it is a light on the detail of what the Sabbath *should* look like.

We do get some clues. The focus of the Sabbath is God, not us. It is an opportunity to recalibrate, to lift our eyes up from the things that preoccupy us the rest of the week, to focus on who God is and what he has called us and the rest of his creation to be.

We also have the freedom to get creative: how, where, when and with whom we choose to focus on God is entirely up to us! As Christians we have sometimes been guilty of occupying a very small box when it comes to the sabbath. Imagine what might happen if we gave ourselves permission to think outside of it.

How might you focus on God today? What are some of the day-to-day preoccupations that might distract you, and what could you do to set them aside, just for today? Where could you go, and who could you spend time with, in order to focus on God?

LOUISE DAVIS

Rest

God saw everything that he had made, and indeed, it was very good. And there was evening and there was morning, the sixth day. Thus the heavens and the earth were finished and all their multitude. On the sixth day God finished the work that he had done, and he rested on the seventh day from all the work that he had done. So God blessed the seventh day and hallowed it, because on it God rested from all the work that he had done in creation.

What constitutes a good holiday is a very personal thing, but I think it is safe to say that one of the priorities for most of us will be taking time to rest and focus on things, people and places that there seem to be little or no time for in day-to-day life.

Yet many of us struggle with rest. We have too many responsibilities, too many balls to juggle. Rest can all too often seem like a luxury. Yet right at the beginning of the Bible, at the heart of this epic account of why the world and humankind came into beginning, we are told that God rested. Having invested of himself for six days, he recognised that it was time to stop.

When life is going well and the things to which I am turning my hands are proving successful, I know that I can all too easily fall into the trap of persuading myself that the sensible thing to do is keep going. Yet in this account of the creation God chooses to rest at his point of greatest success and achievement. He is clearly on a roll: imagine what he could have created if he had just carried on for a couple more days!

Fortunately, God is far wiser than me. That being the case, I really should learn to take a leaf out of his book; if God is able to give himself permission to rest at the point of his greatest productivity, I really should grant myself the same permission.

What are the activities, and who are the people, that enable you to transition into a more restful headspace? Identify one thing that enables you to rest and make space to do that thing today.

LOUISE DAVIS

Sleep

But [Elijah] went a day's journey into the wilderness and came and sat down under a solitary broom tree. He asked that he might die, 'It is enough; now, O Lord, take away my life, for I am no better than my ancestors.' Then he lay down under the broom tree and fell asleep. Suddenly an angel touched him and said to him, 'Get up and eat.' He looked, and there at his head was a cake baked on hot stones and a jar of water. He ate and drank and lay down again.

I will readily concede that today's passage does not immediately appear to fit with the theme of holy days and holidays! And yet how many of us have found ourselves finally going on holiday – or even just taking a few extremely overdue days of annual leave – at the point at which we feel a bit like Elijah, burnt out and exhausted?

Elijah has come to the end of himself and all he can do is curl up in a ball and go to sleep. But in taking that very small, very human step, he inadvertently begins a process of quiet, practical restoration that will enable him to meet with God in a new and powerful way. Sleep is followed by the miraculous provision of food and water, which is followed by more sleep. Which of us has not felt better – even under the most extreme circumstances – after a good meal and an even better sleep?

Many of us struggle with sleep, for myriad different reasons, and yet it is so vital for our health and well-being. While we sleep, our brains go through a complex process of sorting the previous day's experiences, while our bodies are in turn absorbing and transforming the chemicals needed for them to function properly.

What one step could you take today to maximise the potential for a good night's sleep? You might want to consider aiming to go to bed an hour earlier, switching off – or choosing not to use – electronic devices earlier in the evening, or drinking a warm, non-caffeinated drink before bed.
(If, like Elijah, you feel – or have recently felt – that you no longer want to live, it is imperative that you seek professional medical advice.)

LOUISE DAVIS

Hospitality

[Jesus] entered Jericho and was passing through it. A man was there named Zacchaeus; he was a chief tax collector and was rich. He was trying to see who Jesus was, but on account of the crowd he could not, because he was short in stature. So he ran ahead and climbed a sycamore tree to see him, because he was going to pass that way. When Jesus came to the place, he looked up and said to him, 'Zacchaeus, hurry and come down, for I must stay at your house today.' So he hurried down and was happy to welcome him.

The Bible is so full of stories of hospitality and welcome that it is a challenge to pick just one. Growing up in a family that had enough but not much more, my experience of holidays has always tended to be towards the budget end of the spectrum. In fact, the bigger our family became – I ended up as the eldest of four children – the more our holidays tended to revolve around trips to stay with friends and family, bedded down on lilos in sleeping bags, mucking in with cooking, washing up and childcare! But however basic the accommodation, there was never any doubt of the quality of welcome and hospitality we received.

Some of us can find it difficult to accept the hospitality of others, and yet going on holiday requires us to do that, one way or the other. Whether we are staying with friends, renting a self-catering cottage or treating ourselves to a few days in a hotel, we are stepping into someone else's space, becoming the guest rather than the host.

Jesus seemed to share little of our cultural hesitancy about inviting himself to the homes of others or receiving the hospitality he was offered. Today's reading is a great example of this. He understood the importance of receiving hospitality, of stepping into someone else's space and in doing so choosing to experience life from their perspective.

Who could you drop in on today? Consider taking some seasonal flowers, perhaps from your garden, and pop round. If you are invited in, be brave and say yes!

LOUISE DAVIS

Food

Once more Jesus spoke to them in parables, saying: 'The kingdom of heaven may be compared to a king who gave a wedding banquet for his son. He sent his slaves to call those who had been invited to the wedding banquet, but they would not come. Again he sent other slaves, saying, 'Tell those who have been invited: Look, I have prepared my dinner, my oxen and my fat calves have been slaughtered, and everything is ready; come to the wedding banquet.'

When I was growing up, most of our family holidays were spent in self-catering accommodation in which – I now realise – my mum probably had slightly less of a holiday than the rest of us. Yet the specialness of holidays meant that there were edible treats. These included ice cream cones from ice cream vans and, if we were lucky, a cream tea or two shared between the six of us. But one of my most vivid memories is discovering proper Cornish pasties, freshly cooked and eaten warm out of a paper bag sitting on the beach. Another is when the welcome pack from our hosts on a farm in Norfolk included bottles of milk, still warm and fresh from the milking parlour.

It is interesting to reflect on the stories about food we find in the Bible, and there are plenty of them! Many are about God's miraculous provision for his people, but today's reading gives us a different perspective. The wedding banquet in this parable is, as the Anglican Holy Communion liturgy reminds us, a 'foretaste of the heavenly banquet prepared for all peoples'.

Many of us would readily acknowledge that food is one of God's good gifts to us, but I suspect that most of us tend to think about that in terms of the basic food that we need to live on: our literal daily bread. This story reminds us that the food we eat on special occasions, or that we 'ration' for sound practical or financial reasons, is a good gift from God too!

What is your favourite food or your favourite place to eat? If it is practical, why not treat yourself to this meal, or a visit to this place, today? Consider taking one of your favourite people with you or someone you think would value a special invitation.

LOUISE DAVIS

Creation

O Lord, our Sovereign, how majestic is your name in all the earth! You have set your glory above the heavens. Out of the mouths of babes and infants you have founded a bulwark because of your foes, to silence the enemy and the avenger. When I look at your heavens, the work of your fingers, the moon and the stars that you have established; what are human beings that you are mindful of them, mortals that you care for them?

We all have different, very individual criteria by which we judge the ideal holiday destination, but I suspect few of us would choose to spend time somewhere that we did not believe to be in some way beautiful. Unless we are very lucky, most of us will spend at least some of our 'normal life' in environments that are primarily functional rather than beautiful, and travelling on holiday can be a refreshing antidote to this.

That said, beauty is, as we know, in the eye of the beholder. I discovered a couple of years ago that one of my closest friends is passionate about brutalist architecture, so for her a weekend exploring London's South Bank would be the perfect mini-break. In contrast, my perfect weekend away would see me immersed in green, ideally a combination of open countryside and beautiful gardens.

This very familiar psalm is a joyous outpouring of praise to God, triggered by observing the glory and beauty of the natural world, understanding that it all emanates from him and recognising something of the way in which humankind relates to the rest of creation. Might our growing understanding of the interconnectedness of the whole of creation enable us to engage with this psalm with ever greater wonder and delight in the glory and majesty of God?

Whether we prefer a built environment which speaks of the creativity of human endeavour or a more natural landscape – or some combination of the two – most of us will choose to holiday in a place where we can see something of the hand of God at work.

What aspects of creation bring you the most joy? Why is this? Where could you go today to reflect on God's creation? If you're feeling creative, why not try your hand at writing a psalm of praise yourself?

LOUISE DAVIS

New places

Now the Lord said to Abram, 'Go from your country and your kindred and your father's house to the land that I will show you. I will make of you a great nation, and I will bless you and make your name great, so that you will be a blessing. I will bless those who bless you, and the one who curses you I will curse, and in you all the families of the earth shall be blessed.'

In my childhood, my family tended to go on holiday to new places each year. Although our holidays were always in the UK – I have still never been overseas with my family – our summer trips took us to Norfolk, Cornwall, Northumberland and Wales, to name but a few.

Growing up in a busy, noisy south London suburb meant that travelling to and exploring the British countryside sometimes felt akin to discovering a whole new world. Single-track roads replaced the arterial route into central London on which we lived. Open fields unfolded all around us, contrasting with the ubiquitous walls and fences of the town. And the 'country smells' of farms offered a new olfactory experience after the tanneries which – in my childhood – flanked the open mouth of the northbound Blackwall Tunnel.

Journeys and travel are themes which return regularly throughout the Bible, and it is interesting to reflect on the number of individuals in the story of the people of God who are called by God to move out of a place which is familiar and, presumably, relatively comfortable, and go to a new place where they will experience God in new and transformational ways.

When I moved cities almost 15 years ago, I certainly found myself more consciously aware of my need for God's guidance, wisdom and provision. There is something about the 'unknowing' of relocating to a new place that forces us to lean more heavily on God, and, in my personal experience, spiritual growth often follows.

Taking time to think about how our relationship with God has changed and developed can be a really helpful way of exploring how it might continue to grow in the future. Try mapping a timeline of your journey of faith, identifying the people, places and experiences that have shaped it over time.

LOUISE DAVIS

Familiar places

Jacob left Beer-sheba and went towards Haran. He came to a certain place and stayed there for the night, because the sun had set. Taking one of the stones of the place, he put it under his head and lay down in that place. And he dreamed that there was a stairway set up on the earth, the top of it reaching to heaven, and the angels of God were ascending and descending on it… Then Jacob woke from his sleep and said, 'Surely the Lord is in this place—and I did not know it!'

The one area of the UK that became something of an exception to the rule of new summer, new holiday location, was Cornwall. Trips to the South West, which usually began at around 5.00 am in an attempt to miss the south London rush hour, punctuated my childhood and resulted in the holidays that still prompt for me the greatest bouts of reminiscing, decades later.

Celtic Christian spirituality holds the idea of 'thin places', physical places where God seems close, where the gap between heaven and earth seems smaller. While there are particular geographical locations which generations have identified as such places, many of us will have shared something of Jacob's experience at what became known as Bethel, encountering God in a particular place which then takes on a new resonance for us.

Further on in Genesis 28, we read that Jacob took the stone he had slept on and turned it into a physical memorial of his transformational encounter with God, enabling him to ground his experience – which had itself left no physical trace – in something tangible. Many of us will have had experiences of God which have been profound and life-changing, but which have left no physical mark. Personally, I have found that simply writing about those experiences in my journal is sufficient to 'ground' them; for others, creating a more tangible, visible mark is necessary.

Do you have a particular place which is special for you or important in your relationship with God? Why is it important? If you haven't visited it for a while, why not go in the next few days (if it is local) or take some time today to think about the practicalities of prioritising a visit in the next few months?

LOUISE DAVIS

People

Now as they went on their way, he entered a certain village where a woman named Martha welcomed him. She had a sister named Mary, who sat at Jesus' feet and listened to what he was saying. But Martha was distracted by her many tasks, so she came to him and asked, 'Lord, do you not care that my sister has left me to do all the work by myself? Tell her, then, to help me.' But the Lord answered her, 'Martha, Martha, you are worried and distracted by many things, but few things are needed – indeed only one. Mary has chosen the better part, which will not be taken away from her.

It is perfectly possible to have a lovely holiday on your own. In February 2020, before we had any lockdowns, as news of a terrible virus sweeping China began to burrow itself into our collective consciousness, I went alone to Buxton in Derbyshire for my first holiday in 15 years. I spent five glorious days in a tiny cottage, reading, eating nice food and sleeping: a lot. It snowed and as I left, feeling refreshed and reinvigorated, it took me two attempts to leave the village.

There is, however, something special and important about sharing holidays with others, particularly with people we do not see every day. While we often most closely associate Jesus with his twelve disciples, it is clear from the gospels that he also had close friends to whom he was deeply attached. Mary, Martha and Lazarus are great examples of such friends, a family in whose home Jesus was a valued guest. When Lazarus died, the shortest verse in the Bible simply tells us that 'Jesus wept' (John 11:35, NIV).

Who are the people you are closest to or value the most? When was the last time you spent quality time with them? Why not arrange to have dinner together or go out for the day? Perhaps there is someone you have spent a little time with but would like to get to know better. Take the bull by the horns and suggest meeting them for coffee.

LOUISE DAVIS

Conversation

Now before the festival of the Passover, Jesus knew that his hour had come to depart from this world and go to the Father. Having loved his own who were in the world, he loved them to the end… After Jesus had spoken these words, he went out with his disciples across the Kidron Valley to a place where there was a garden, which he and his disciples entered.

Doing things while on holiday is all very well, but sometimes the not doing, the just being, is as important. Holidays create space for conversation and the sharing of ideas. When we feel more relaxed, it can be easier to be a little more vulnerable, to give a bit more of ourselves.

Of the 21 chapters of John's gospel, he sets aside five – just under a quarter of the entire book – to his account of Jesus' final meal with his disciples. If ever there was a conversation that would change the world, this was it.

Many of us will have found ourselves sitting late into the night, perhaps over good food or a glass of something, talking with friends and family to a depth and with a purpose which rarely feels possible at home. Those conversations – and indeed those occasions – can inevitably become fewer and further between when the pressures and obligations of normal life intrude.

It is important to notice that sharing the Passover with his disciples was an occasion for which Jesus had planned. He was intentional about wanting to spend this time with his trusted group of friends, and he wasn't leaving things to chance. Occasions when we set aside unhurried time with people who are important to us can be worth their weight in gold.

When was the last time you had a really 'deep and meaningful' conversation with a close friend, members of your family or maybe even your significant other? Why not take the opportunity to create some quality conversation time with someone important that you haven't talked to for a while? Ideally aim to do this in person, but sometimes constraints of time or geography can make that difficult; the conversation itself is more important than the location!

LOUISE DAVIS

Past

Now on that same day two of them were going to a village called Emmaus, about seven miles from Jerusalem, and talking with each other about all these things that had happened. While they were talking and discussing, Jesus himself came near and went with them, but their eyes were kept from recognising him. And he said to them, 'What are you discussing with each other while you walk along?'

When I was growing up, my family were members of the National Trust and English Heritage, so no holiday was complete without trips to glorious houses, castles and gardens within a 45-minute travel time of our self-catering cottage. Visiting these extraordinary places had two long-lasting impacts on me. First, they enabled me to come face-to-face with the kind of beauty, skill, creativity and vision that were somewhat lacking in my day-to-day suburban existence. Second, they gave me a tangible sense of the national story into which I had been born and was growing up.

In the period over which I have been visiting heritage properties, our collective understanding of the importance of knowing *who* is telling 'our' story has grown and developed significantly. There is now a growing recognition that we need to tell the story of *everyone* who has shaped who we are as a nation, not just the stories of those with power and money.

Today's reading reminds us of the importance of reading the story of God's people through the eyes of the person on whom it is centred. These two grieving friends couldn't make sense of the events they had witnessed until Jesus unpacked it with them. He was a master storyteller, and he uses those skills to stunning effect as he walks and talks with his friends. He weaves a narrative that reaches back into the story of the people of God, the places they have inhabited, the divine encounters they have had, until in a moment of true theatre he re-enacts the giving of the bread and the wine and the last supper and, in this moment, 'their eyes were opened, and they recognised him, and he vanished from their sight' (Luke 24:31).

Do you ever take time to think about the people, places and experience that have shaped you? How has your perception of those things changed over time?

LOUISE DAVIS

Journalling

Mary said, 'My soul magnifies the Lord, and my spirit rejoices in God my Saviour, for he has looked with favour on the lowly state of his servant. Surely from now on all generations will call me blessed, for the Mighty One has done great things for me, and holy is his name; indeed, his mercy is for those who fear him from generation to generation. He has shown strength with his arm; he has scattered the proud in the imagination of their hearts. He has brought down the powerful from their thrones and lifted up the lowly; he has filled the hungry with good things and sent the rich away empty.'

One of the first things that goes in my suitcase whenever I go away on holiday is my journal. As I journal on those occasions, I often find myself looking back over longer periods of time and, for example, seeing connections between events or experiences that I have previously overlooked.

I have a sneaking suspicion that had Mary been born at a time when pen and paper (and education for girls) were freely available, she would have been an inveterate journal-er. The first two chapters of Luke portray a young woman who thought deeply about the encounters she had – whether with angels or shepherds – and took time to process their significance.

It can be tempting to read this glorious passage from Luke as a spontaneous outpouring of praise, and perhaps it was. But I suspect that from the moment of her encounter with Gabriel, Mary had been processing the experience and making connections with what appears to be a deep-rooted understanding of the history and call of her nation.

What is important here is not the method of reflection – journalling is just one way in which to process experience – but the value of reflection itself. Holidays can offer vital space and time in which to reflect on our own experiences.

If you keep a journal or diary, why not dig out a notebook from a few years ago and take the opportunity to reflect back on an earlier part of your life? If you do not regularly journal, consider buying a nice notebook and pen and experiment with recording your thoughts and reflections on this fortnight of daily readings.

LOUISE DAVIS

Languages

When the day of Pentecost had come, they were all together in one place. And suddenly from heaven there came a sound like the rush of a violent wind, and it filled the entire house where they were sitting. Divided tongues, as of fire, appeared among them, and a tongue rested on each of them. All of them were filled with the Holy Spirit and began to speak in other languages, as the Spirit gave them ability.

Holidays can be a great opportunity to get to know a new culture and a new language. And we do not even need to leave the UK to do so. Fifteen years ago, I moved from London to Leicestershire, initially to the county and then into the city of Leicester itself. It had not occurred to me that I might need to make some language adjustments, until I discovered cobs and jitties!

Leicester is, famously, one of the most diverse cities in the UK and my own experience of living here has reflected that. I live in rented accommodation in a less-than-salubrious area of the city with a relatively high population turnover. In the six years I have lived here, my neighbours have included Italian Muslims, Pakistani Christians, a lovely Polish couple, and students and their families from Kerala in India, living alongside the white British families who have populated this area for generations.

Shared language is a significant part of building good relationships, and most of my neighbours have, entirely predictably and regardless of country of origin, spoken excellent English, putting my own limited foreign language skills to shame! But we have also had to resort to sign language and Google Translate at times, and I learnt very quickly that a broad grin goes a long way when it comes to building good relationships.

Who in your day-to-day life do you need to communicate better with?
How might you temper your own default modes of communication?
What can you do to help others communicate better with you?

LOUISE DAVIS

Sabbath revisited

If you refrain from trampling the Sabbath, from pursuing your own interests on my holy day; if you call the Sabbath a delight and the holy day of the Lord honourable; if you honour it, not going your own ways, serving your own interests or pursuing your own affairs; then you shall take delight in the Lord, and I will make you ride upon the heights of the earth; I will feed you with the heritage of your ancestor Jacob, for the mouth of the Lord has spoken.

The reality of all holidays is that they come to an end! Many of us will know the feeling of heading home after a week of rest, relaxation, good food and good company, determined to make changes that will mean that something of that holiday spirit will continue as we re-enter 'normal life'. All of us know just how hard it is to do that in reality.

We began this series of reflections with a reading from Exodus which reminded us that the sabbath is a holy day, set apart by God for rest and to give us space to recalibrate our perspective, refocusing on who God is and who he has called us to be.

Today we have come full circle, and we end with this challenging reminder from Isaiah which helps us to consider what it might mean to ensure that our holy days continue to impact our every day. Isaiah is reminding God's people that a true sabbath means refocusing on God and honouring his day. But he also reminds them that the values and principles of sabbath, of making sure God keeps his rightful place in our activities and relationships, does not stop when the sabbath ends. The other six days of the week should also be days when God's kingdom values – grace, justice, mercy, compassion – shape our lives, our choices and our relationships.

Think back over the elements of a holiday that you have thought about over the last two weeks. What do you want to commit to taking with you back into 'normal life'? How will you build rest, quality 'people time', good food, travel and reflection on your own story into the days to come?

How might you commit to putting God's kingdom values –
grace, justice, mercy, compassion – into practice in the everyday?

LOUISE DAVIS

Song of Songs

 I remember well my first introduction to the Song of Songs (or Song of Solomon). A friend, all nudge-nudge-wink-wink, pointed out the pages in our not-yet-well-worn Bibles and we giggled to ourselves over the sexual references and preposterous descriptions of love.

Song of Songs is unique, for sure. Classified as wisdom literature, it is an extended love poem containing the same visceral rawness as some of the Psalms. The focus is not directly upon God, however. Instead, its cyclic themes offer an unashamed outpouring regarding human sexuality.

Despite the frequent references to Solomon, the book was more likely penned in honour of the king than by him. The English Standard Version (ESV), which I have used for these reflections, dates it to around 961–931BC, before Israel was divided into the northern and southern kingdoms, whereas other commentators suggest somewhere between the fifth and third centuries BC. Far more pressing, though, are the reasons for writing it.

Interpretations have varied across the centuries and church traditions. It can be read as presented – a celebration of sexual love, with all its yearnings, fears of loss and eventual consummation – or as an allegory – a depiction of God's love for his people or of Christ the bridegroom loving the church.

I would suggest that there are problems with either of these approaches. If we limit our focus to the human love story, we should question why we ought to study it at all. Part of the answer, of course, is that we get a greater understanding of the Bible's clear stance on sex being confined within the marriage covenant. As Eugene Peterson says in *The Message*: 'The Song proclaims an integrated wholeness that is at the centre of Christian teaching on committed, wedded love for a world that seems to specialise in loveless sex.'

If, on the other hand, we see the book purely as allegory, one could argue why the content needs to be so explicit. The idea of God wanting to be committedly intimate with his people is wonderful, but I guess we might squirm if we stretch the metaphors too far.

Over the next few days, I shall try to keep a balanced consideration in order to draw us closer to the God, who pursues us and whose love for us cannot be rivalled.

JANE WALTERS

Intimacy with God

The Song of Songs, which is Solomon's. [She] Let him kiss me with the kisses of his mouth! For your love is better than wine; your anointing oils are fragrant; your name is oil poured out; therefore virgins love you. Draw me after you; let us run. The king has brought me into his chambers. [Others] We will exult and rejoice in you; we will extol your love more than wine; rightly do they love you.

The opening verses of Song of Songs (a phrase that means the best of songs, along the same lines as 'king of kings') might seem familiar from our church worship. I remember singing, 'I will rejoice in you and be glad, I will extol your love more than wine,' long before the days when I was legally allowed to drink! But perhaps an old memory is a reminder of the timelessness of this book's themes: the longing and passion of the beloved for her lover and his enjoyment of her. In the background are the 'others', acting as cheerleaders watching the unfolding drama: a reminder perhaps of how we are 'surrounded by so great a cloud of witnesses' (Hebrews 12:1).

The young woman here is not holding back in her anticipation of her lover. She is intoxicated by everything about him, even the way he smells and the sound of his voice. If we are to consider this passage in terms of us expressing our love for God, we might feel that it is altogether too much. Perhaps it might surprise you to know that the Greek word for 'worship' is *proskuneo*, which means 'to kiss', with connotations of bowing or kneeling before a superior to do so.

Her use of the phrase 'draw me after you' (v. 4) is a reminder that Jesus takes the initiative with us. We often refer to people looking into faith as 'seeking'. It is truer to say, however, that we have a God who seeks us. 'You did not choose me, but I chose you,' Jesus says (John 15:16). We love because the Lover first loved us.

Jesus, your love draws me and compels me to fall at your feet in worship. Reveal more of yourself to me so that I may love you more fully and worship you more wholeheartedly. Amen.

JANE WALTERS

Fulfilled anticipation

The voice of my beloved! Behold, he comes, leaping over the mountains, bounding over the hills. My beloved is like a gazelle or a young stag. Behold, there he stands behind our wall, gazing through the windows, looking through the lattice. My beloved speaks and says to me: 'Arise, my love, my beautiful one, and come away, for behold, the winter is past; the rain is over and gone. The flowers appear on the earth, the time of singing has come, and the voice of the turtle-dove is heard in our land.'

The woman is expressively eloquent again, this time in describing her anticipation. Yesterday, we read how she loved the man's scent and his name; here just the recall of his voice is enough to set her a-quiver! But her anticipation is not a hollow yearning, a wishful thinking. Already, her lover is on his way, taking ground in great strides in his own eagerness to be with her.

I must admit that I have not always been as diligent as I could be over my daily quiet time. Sometimes, despite my best intentions, the demands of the day shout louder than the gentle, inviting whispers of my Saviour. I remember a time, some years ago, when I realised how much I was missing Jesus! I knelt in prayer, nose almost pressed to the carpet, and poured out my longing for him on paper, my tears splashing the page. This is what love can look like: the ache to reconnect, to say, 'I've missed you. Come close again.'

And how does our Lord respond? By turning up so quickly that it is as if he has taken one giant bound to reach us. (Of course, the greater truth is that he never left our side, though it can feel as if he did.) In his swift arrival is an invitation to get up and join him, to put behind the things that have kept us from his presence and to embrace all that lies ahead.

Jesus, away from you it feels like a permanent winter.
Come close to me now and put fresh hope into my heart. Amen.

JANE WALTERS

Watch out for pests!

'The fig tree ripens its figs, and the vines are in blossom; they give forth fragrance. Arise, my love, my beautiful one, and come away. O my dove, in the clefts of the rock, In the crannies of the cliff, let me see your face, let me hear your voice, for your voice is sweet, and your face is lovely. Catch the foxes for us, the little foxes that spoil the vineyards, for our vineyards are in blossom.'

Nearly three years ago, the church I attend bought a former factory in the middle of town. Along with the massive renovations needed to turn the derelict industrial buildings into a worship centre and community amenities, the surrounding landscape also had to be reclaimed. A team of volunteers worked hard to conquer acres of brambles and self-set saplings. However, one issue remained: the presence of muntjac deer, who proceeded to chomp their way through every attempt at planting bulbs, flowers and shrubs.

Any form of progress will have its opposition. Whether it's the natural world, with its weeds, pests and predators, or development within our own lives, we know only too well that the path can be both slippery and filled with obstacles. The lovers in this book have been rejoicing in their love, caught up in the glory of it; and yet the very vineyards that have spoken of fruitfulness and potential celebration are under threat from 'the little foxes'.

In almost every story of a fall from grace or a descent into sin of any kind, tiny steps were taken which should have been avoided. It is rarely one inciting event – the equivalent of a lion pouncing – but a series of smaller ones – the little foxes – that do the damage. As our story shows, the great love these two have for one another is not sufficient protection against life's ravages. Our church outwitted the deer by surrounding the tender specimens with wire netting. I wonder what tactics you might deploy against the little munchers in your own life?

Jesus, I am grateful for the ways your love blesses me and enriches my life. Help me guard myself against even the most subtle attempts of the enemy to spoil what you are creating. Help me be vigilant as well as thankful. Amen.

JANE WALTERS

In pursuit of true love

The watchmen found me as they went about in the city. 'Have you seen him whom my soul loves?' Scarcely had I passed them when I found him whom my soul loves. I held him, and would not let him go until I had brought him into my mother's house, and into the chamber of her who conceived me. I adjure you, O daughters of Jerusalem, by the gazelles or the does of the field, that you not stir up or awaken love until it pleases.

If you have ever lost something, you will understand the kind of madness that can descend as you search anywhere and everywhere to find it. While forgetting where I left my glasses is a daily nuisance, losing an item of value provokes more than irritation; the situation can feel desperate. I still remember the utter relief of finding – almost miraculously – a ruby that had fallen out of a ring. I simply could not rest until I had located it.

In today's verses, the woman is dreaming. Once more, she is yearning for the one whom her soul loves. It is not enough that she lies in bed with thoughts of him in her head. Her desire prompts her to action and she imagines herself searching high and low through the streets of the city. The watchmen are no help, but she is undeterred. When she does eventually find him, she grips him tightly so as not to lose him a second time and brings him to her childhood home, a place of refuge and safety.

I am reminded of some words of St Augustine of Hippo: 'You have made us for yourself, O Lord, and our heart is restless until it finds its rest in you.' Along with many millions of others, we can try to meet our needs by cramming our lives full of busyness, material possessions and all kinds of numbing substances. It is only when we come to realise that our deepest need is a spiritual one that we can let go of all the 'stuff' and seek the one our souls crave. All our searching is satisfied when we find him, and we should do well never to let him go!

Jesus, you are the one our souls love.
We need you, we seek you, please be near. Amen.

JANE WALTERS

Love to the exclusion of others

A garden locked is my sister, my bride, a spring locked, a fountain sealed. Your shoots are an orchard of pomegranates with all choicest fruits, henna with nard, nard and saffron, calamus and cinnamon, with all trees of frankincense, myrrh and aloes, with all choice spices – a garden fountain, a well of living water, and flowing streams from Lebanon. Awake, O north wind, and come, O south wind! Blow upon my garden, let its spices flow.

When I read this chapter, I cannot help compare the rather pathetic – though admirably romantic – strewing of rose petals on a marital bed to this lush description of a veritable Kew Gardens. The marriage between the man and woman is imminent, with its promise of loving consummation. The imagery of their bodies, expounded in the verses surrounding today's text, would be laughable if we did not appreciate the lengths to which the couple were going to articulate their utter admiration of each other. Likewise, the descriptions of this garden are somewhat over the top, but we get the idea.

Creation began in a garden. Eden was the most superlative example there has ever been: a riot of exotic plants, offering a sensory overload of colour and scent, thriving effortlessly in the perfect, sinless environment. Not a weed in sight! And what of its fruitfulness – the sense that these plants would be there for eternity, waxing and waning with the seasons but gloriously productive? This was the setting for the first human love story, between Adam and Eve; and here, in this depiction of the two young lovers, we see God's love for us, his bride, the church.

In the ten commandments, God describes himself as a jealous God (Exodus 20:5) who tolerates no rivals. The description of the 'garden locked… spring locked… fountain sealed' (v. 12) conveys the exclusivity of love. In a real sense, only the lover holds the key. Many things and people in this world vie for our attention and our affection. Do we too, so caught up in the glories around us, miss the presence of our lover entirely, metaphorically speaking?

God, we love you and marvel that you could love us as extravagantly as you do. We want to fix our devotion on you and you alone. Amen.

JANE WALTERS

Love: the most awesome word of all

You are beautiful as Tirzah, my love, lovely as Jerusalem, awesome as an army with banners. Turn away your eyes from me, for they overwhelm me – Your hair is like a flock of goats leaping down the slopes of Gilead… The young women saw her and called her blessed; the queens and concubines also, and they praised her. 'Who is this who looks down like the dawn, beautiful as the moon, bright as the sun, awesome as an army with banners?'

Our readings so far have acclimatised us to the extravagant outpourings of the lovers as they take increasing delight in each other. Exhausting the pool of nature's earthly beauty, he now compares her to Israel's most important cities and then, when this proves inadequate all over again, he turns his gaze to the sky. 'You are out of this world,' he is saying. But what of the curious reference to 'an army with banners' (v. 10)?

A banner has already been mentioned in 2:4: 'He brought me to the banqueting house, and his banner over me was love,' no doubt referring to the public declaration of his love. However, in this chapter we have the added detail of 'an army with banners'. An army would go into battle with banners fluttering, identifying itself both as a whole and in its individual sections. Imagine the scene: each opposing side approaching the other, with roars of defiance and perhaps the sound of drumbeats. As they come nearer, the banners are all the more visible; their slogans and motifs announcing their confidence, intent on striking fear into hearts.

Here is where the word 'awesome' comes into its own, for one message stands above them all: love. God's banner over us is love, and he ever holds it in place for all to see. It reminds me of Isaiah 59:19: 'When the enemy shall come in like a flood, the Spirit of the Lord shall lift up a standard against him' (KJV).

Love can overcome every enemy. Love always prevails. Love always wins.

Jesus, you are the victor, reigning supreme because of your death-defying sacrifice on the cross. Let me share your love with everyone I meet today, helping push back their darkness and ushering in your kingdom. Amen.

JANE WALTERS

The power of love

Set me as a seal on your heart, as a seal upon your arm, for love is strong as death, jealousy is fierce as the grave. Its flashes are flashes of fire, the very flame of the Lord. Many waters cannot quench love, neither can floods drown it. If a man offered for love all the wealth of his house, he would be utterly despised.

On our final day exploring the Song of Songs, we read these impassioned words from the woman, whose intense longing has been expressed with increasing strength throughout the story. Now they are married and what more can be said, other than these pleas for permanence?

All along I have aimed for a balanced approach so we can treat this book both as a human love story and as an allegory depicting God's love for us, the church, his bride. Here is the first direct mention of God and, I suggest, it is only in him that we find the longevity and security of love that we crave. He is, after all, a covenant-making God who always keeps his promises.

The 'seal' likely means a ring to be worn on the finger but could also refer to a gold cylinder worn around the neck. Either way, the idea behind it is clear: she wants both the intimacy of being kept in his heart and the public demonstration of belonging to him. In similar vein, Paul teaches that God 'has also put his seal on us and given us his Spirit in our hearts as a guarantee' (2 Corinthians 1:22). In a real sense, God has claimed us for his own and provided the proof that he has done so.

Love – not mere lust or sex – has been this book's predominant theme. Love, in its truest sense, emanates from God, the ultimate flame which produces all subsequent sparks. He holds love as a banner over us and sustains it in the face of opposition. Fire cannot consume it, floodwater cannot overwhelm it and jealous devotion will protect it. Love never fails.

God of love, may we receive your love with ever thankful hearts.
Cleanse us from the sin that would distort this most precious gift
so we can share it with others and draw them to you. Amen.

JANE WALTERS

Revelation 10—18

Revelation chapters 10 to 18 encompass most of what people mean when they describe it as a 'difficult' book of the Bible. There are exciting scenes of heavenly conflict and angelic triumph, but also fearful images of judgement and destruction. Taken out of context, some passages sound as if they have been lifted straight from a fantasy novel or horror film. There are stirring themes of light conquering darkness – and troubling passages about judgement that appears indiscriminate in its violence. It's no surprise that the popular verdict on Revelation can sometimes be 'leave well alone'!

Picking a way through John the Evangelist's tumultuous visions can certainly be hard work, but Revelation is not the only part of the Bible to showcase the kind of writing known as 'apocalyptic'. While that word is now understood as 'relating to the end of the world', the original Greek word meant 'revelation' (hence the name of the book). The 'Apocalypse' of John meant the series of visions that John received on the island of Patmos, visions that revealed the spiritual realities behind the earthly powers of the age.

Turning to the later chapters of the book of Daniel, we find imagery and themes similar to Revelation and there are further examples in the gospels and the prophets. The temptation is to try to read these as predications of the future, with easy identification of the 'beast' with the current global 'evil empire' (whatever our political outlook). Turning away from sensationalist and pseudo-prophetic interpretations, we can end up mired in textual analysis, trying to make sense of what has intrigued and puzzled commentators for 2,000 years.

These readings offer a more devotional approach, sampling some of the best-known passages and tracing overarching themes of God's sustaining care and mercy. Such themes will help to guide us through the many twists and turns of Revelation. As we read we can also hold in mind the vision of eternal worship found in chapter 4, the unceasing praise of 'the Lord God the Almighty, who was and is and is to come'. Let that praise ring in our ears and reassure us if the threat of darkness ever seems greater than the promise of the light!

NAOMI STARKEY

The sweet and the bitter

Then the voice… spoke to me again, saying, 'Go, take the scroll that is open in the hand of the angel who is standing on the sea and on the land.' So I went to the angel and told him to give me the little scroll, and he said to me, 'Take it and eat; it will be bitter to your stomach but sweet as honey in your mouth.' So I took the little scroll… and ate it; it was sweet as honey in my mouth, but when I had eaten it my stomach was made bitter. Then they said to me, 'You must prophesy again about many peoples and nations and languages and kings.'

The angels we meet in Revelation bear little resemblance to the heavenly creatures of popular imagination. There is nothing sweet, pretty or indeed feathery about these giant, shining beings whose appearances are heralded by what sound like volcanic eruptions. Earlier in this chapter, we hear of an angel whose shout is like a lion roaring, a spine-tingling, ground-quaking noise that is totally different from the usual notion of 'angelic voices'. Unsurprisingly, John the narrator is obedient to these roaring voices, no matter how bizarre the command may seem (and the prophet Ezekiel had a similar experience, centuries before).

Amid this upheaval, he receives a scroll that gives him his prophetic task. He literally has to consume the message – relieved, presumably, that it is a 'little scroll' – but discovers that (as we might say) it 'turns his stomach'. His task is a source both of blessing and of bitterness. That may come as a surprise to us, familiar as we are with the idea of faith as connection with God's love, forgiveness and mercy. Here we are reminded of how the gospel is also a means of division and pain, as Jesus himself spoke of bringing not peace 'but a sword' (Matthew 10:34). Letting in the light shows up the dirt and darkness, and that can be a bitter experience.

Pray for those you know whose gifting and responsibility involves preaching, that they will be able to balance proclaiming forgiveness with naming of sin, the blessing with the bitterness.

NAOMI STARKEY

Found: that which was lost

Then the seventh angel blew his trumpet, and there were loud voices in heaven, saying, 'The kingdom of the world has become the kingdom of our Lord and of his Messiah, and he will reign forever and ever.' Then the twenty-four elders who sit on their thrones before God fell on their faces and worshipped God, singing... Then God's temple in heaven was opened, and the ark of his covenant was seen within his temple; and there were flashes of lightning, rumblings, peals of thunder, an earthquake, and heavy hail.

I wonder how many *New Daylight* readers remember the film *Raiders of the Lost Ark*? Steven Spielberg's wartime adventure reaches a crescendo of excitement when the ark (which in the film is indeed the long-lost ark of the covenant) is opened by a greedy archaeologist, directed by a bunch of Nazis hoping to access limitless power. No spoilers for anyone who has not seen it, but the baddies come to an appropriately nasty end.

The Bible does not speak of what befell the ark of the covenant, that most sacred object and symbol of God's presence with his people. It simply disappears at the time of the exile to Babylon. Wonderfully, in John's vision, it is revealed as back where it was always intended to be: at the heart of the temple. Although the ark remains closed, the temple's opening is accompanied by dramatic phenomena that would have signalled to Revelation's original audience that here was God's very presence.

Notice the numbers in this reading: the seventh (meaning completion or perfection) angel blows his trumpet and the 24 elders (perhaps symbolising the twelve tribes of Israel plus twelve apostles) worship God. In the intricate code language of Revelation, these numbers are woven into John's vision to emphasise that the culmination of history is unshakeably in the hands of the creator of history. We need not be afraid, however unnerving the signs of the times. When the smoke clears and the storms cease, every eye will see and every heart will finally recognise the Lord of all.

What precious thing or person would you long to see,
once lost but now found safe in God's holy dwelling place?

NAOMI STARKEY

Here be dragons

A great portent appeared in heaven: a woman clothed with the sun, with the moon under her feet, and on her head a crown of twelve stars. She was pregnant and was crying out in birth pangs, in the agony of giving birth. Then another portent appeared in heaven: a great red dragon, with seven heads and ten horns and seven diadems on his heads... Then the dragon stood before the woman who was about to deliver a child, so that he might devour her child as soon as it was born. And she gave birth to a son, a male child, who is to rule all the nations with a sceptre of iron.

For anyone in Wales, mention of the red dragon is likely to bring to mind the national flag. In Revelation, though, the red dragon is the embodiment of evil. Its seven heads signify complete or total wickedness, while the description of 'ten horns' links to the terrible dragon described in Daniel 7.

The scene is terrifying: a woman cries out in the anguish of labour, disabled by pain despite her celestial adornments. Before her stands the dreadful dragon, jaws gaping to snatch its prey even as the baby draws his first breath. The words 'And she gave birth to a son' take us straight to the birth of Jesus, but this woman is more than a type of Mary. There are echoes of Eve, mother of humanity whose offspring would destroy the 'serpent' (another dragon-like being). There are also echoes of ancient stories from other Near Eastern cultures, sharing similar themes of light and life overcoming darkness and death.

We know that 'the dragon' did not devour the baby Jesus, who survived threatened assassination and exile to grow to maturity and do his Father's work in the world. But today's powerfully dramatic reading is a reminder of the spiritual realities behind the familiar story of the first Christmas. The almighty God truly risked everything in sending his Son to be born as one of us.

Pray for women giving birth today in countries where pregnancy and labour still risk maternal and infant death.

NAOMI STARKEY

War in heaven

And war broke out in heaven; Michael and his angels fought against the dragon. The dragon and his angels fought back, but they were defeated, and there was no longer any place for them in heaven. The great dragon was thrown down, that ancient serpent, who is called the devil and Satan, the deceiver of the whole world – he was thrown down to the earth, and his angels were thrown down with him... [and] he pursued the woman who had delivered the male child. But the woman was given the two wings of the great eagle, so that she could fly from the serpent into the wilderness.

This scene is worthy of any Hollywood blockbuster: there is war, dark and light angels, a 'great dragon' and a woman literally flying with eagle's wings 'into the wilderness'. In Jewish thought, Michael was the chief (or 'arch') angel; he also appears in the book of Daniel and, along with Gabriel, is one of only two of God's messengers (which is what 'angel' means) named in the Bible. And in case things were not quite clear, the link between dragon, serpent, devil, Satan and deceiver is spelled out: this conflict is about the light and power of God overcoming the darkness and disruption that has sought to damage God's purposes since the very beginning.

The description of 'war in heaven' seems, at first, the stuff of nightmares: is this battleground what awaits us beyond the grave? We should note, however, that here, 'heaven' simply indicates 'spiritual realm' – in other words, the cosmic conflict has taken place outside any earthly dimension.

Most importantly, this conflict is finished; darkness has been defeated. God acted decisively, once and for all, in the death and resurrection of Jesus. That physical embodiment of the cosmic conflict has bought forgiveness for the whole of humanity. The taunts of the accuser – that we are 'not good enough for God' – need no longer have any power over us.

'Therefore there is now no condemnation for those who are in Christ Jesus. For the law of the Spirit of life in Christ Jesus has set you free from the law of sin and of death' (Romans 8:1–2).

NAOMI STARKEY

The number of the beast

Then I saw another beast that rose out of the earth; it had two horns like a lamb, and it spoke like a dragon… it causes all, both small and great, both rich and poor, both free and slave, to be given a brand on the right hand or the forehead, so that no one can buy or sell who does not have the brand, that is, the name of the beast or the number for its name. This calls for wisdom: let anyone with understanding calculate the number of the beast, for it is the number of a person. Its number is six hundred sixty-six.

The idea of 'the number of the beast' has spread far and wide in popular culture and, along with the number 13, is considered an evil omen and enduring basis for conspiracy theories. We should heed the call for 'wisdom' and note that 666 is part of the specific coded language of Revelation. It could be interpreted as 'Nero Caesar' or 'beast' or simply 'three times less than perfection' (we might say 'imperfection cubed'), since seven indicated perfection or completion according to the conventions of this style of writing. Six falls short of perfection.

The beast here is also the second of two beasts in this chapter. The first emerges from the sea and appears to have survived a mortal wound, a miracle that brings the nations to worship it. The second beast, coming out of the earth, looks like a lamb (suggesting innocence and goodness) but speaks 'like a dragon' (and we know the true identity of the dragon). It extends the power of the first beast and, with its number or brand, controls the marketplace.

Jesus spoke forcefully and frequently about the deceptive power of wealth, which holds out the false promise that a fulfilled, perfected life can be bought and sold like any commodity. Rather than worrying about a 666 house number or car registration, we would do better to apply some wise thinking to the ways we use – and are used by – the economic systems of our world.

'It is easier for a camel to go through the eye of a needle than for someone who is rich to enter the kingdom of God' (Mark 10:25).

NAOMI STARKEY

In praise of the Lamb

Then I looked, and there was the Lamb, standing on Mount Zion! And with him were one hundred forty-four thousand who had his name and his Father's name written on their foreheads. And I heard a voice from heaven like the sound of many waters and like the sound of loud thunder; the voice I heard was like the sound of harpists playing on their harps, and they sing a new song before the throne and before the four living creatures and before the elders. No one could learn that song except the one hundred forty-four thousand who have been redeemed from the earth.

After the dragon and beasts it is a wonderful relief to return to a vision of glory. The revelations to John began with the appearance of a dazzling figure 'like the Son of Man' (1:13) who tells him not to be afraid. Now, after the fearsome parade of deception and evil, we are reminded of the heavenly reality: the mark of the beast is countered by the mark that is the name of God, indelibly identifying those who are safe in his keeping.

The 144,000 are another symbol (of the many in Revelation) of God's people, the church, gathered to praise and serve the Lamb who has saved them. The 'voice from heaven' is the voice of God, louder, sweeter and stronger than any earthly music, and it calls forth praise from the gathered host that is a 'new song'. It is only those who have experienced God's redeeming love who can even learn that song, because God's love and self-sacrifice is beyond human imagining; it can only be received in humility and honoured in worship.

Our acts of worship, week by week, may employ the most highly trained choir or the most professional band – or they may be entirely homemade and hesitant. Every note is still caught up in that glorious, eternal chorus; every word is still heard and treasured by the one whom we praise.

'"Worthy the Lamb that died," they cry, "to be exalted thus!" "Worthy the Lamb," our lips reply, "for he was slain for us!"' (Isaac Watts, 1674–1748).

NAOMI STARKEY

Harvest of blood

Then another angel came out of the temple in heaven, and he, too, had a sharp sickle. Then another angel came out from the altar, the angel who has authority over fire, and he called with a loud voice… 'Use your sharp sickle and gather the clusters of the vine of the earth, for its grapes are ripe.' So the angel swung his sickle over the earth and gathered the vintage of the earth, and he threw it into the great winepress of the wrath of God. And the winepress was trodden outside the city, and blood flowed from the winepress.

This is the second of two sorts of reaping in chapter 14. The harvest of 'the vintage of the earth' comes after verses describing how 'one like the Son of Man' appears on the clouds and also reaps the earth with a 'sharp sickle'. While John is not told what happens to the first harvest, the fate of the second is graphically described in terms of blood flowing from the 'wine press of the wrath of God' to flood a vast area.

We may well struggle to work out whether this passage is supposed to be a warning ('Watch out or you may be caught up in this!') or a celebration of victory ('See how God destroys the forces of evil!'). There are hints of Isaiah 63, where a warrior appears clothed in 'red… garments like theirs who tread the winepress' and tells of how he has 'trodden the winepress alone' (vv. 2–3). At the same time, the mention of wine and blood calls to mind the wine of the new covenant, poured out in remembrance of the blood of Christ that was shed 'outside the city', which is where the 'winepress of the wrath of God' stands. The poetry of Revelation may defy tidy interpretation, but its energy can still stir our hearts.

'He said to them: "This is my blood of the covenant, which is poured out for many… I will never again drink of the fruit of the vine until that day when I drink it new in the kingdom of God"' (Mark 14:24–25).

NAOMI STARKEY

Songs of praise

Then I saw another portent in heaven, great and amazing: seven angels with seven plagues, which are the last, for with them the wrath of God is ended. And I saw what appeared to be a sea of glass mixed with fire and those who had conquered the beast and its image and the number of its name standing beside the sea of glass with harps of God in their hands. And they sing the song of Moses, the servant of God, and the song of the Lamb: 'Great and amazing are your deeds, Lord God the Almighty! Just and true are your ways, King of the nations!'

The 'portent in heaven' revealed in these verses emphasises the dream-like quality of Revelation, discomforting those who prefer narratives in logical, cause-and-effect order! John is shown 'seven angels with seven plagues', who will conclude God's judgement on evil and rebellion. In the very next sentence there is another scene of triumphant praise, with reference to the 'song of Moses' as well as the 'song of the Lamb'. Perhaps the latter is the 'new song' we have already considered (see 9 August). The Old Testament has three 'songs of Moses' (Exodus 15; Deuteronomy 32; Psalm 90), but the song mentioned here surely refers to the Exodus hymn of praise, with its theme of deliverance.

Traditional 'hellfire and brimstone' preaching makes much of plagues and punishments, but terrifying people into making a faith commitment gives a wholly distorted impression of our God, who 'so loved the world that he gave his only Son, so that everyone who believes in him may not perish but may have eternal life' (John 3:16). There is always a balance to strike between, on the one hand, God's anger at sin and at the devastation it causes and, on the other, God's passionate love for us, his sinful children. That passionate love is the source from which God's supreme act of deliverance springs: the giving of the 'Lamb of God who takes away the sin of the world' (John 1:29). It's no wonder that the heavenly hymns of praise resound without end.

'Holy, Holy, Holy! All the saints adore thee, casting down their golden crowns around the glassy sea' (Reginald Heber, 1783–1826).

NAOMI STARKEY

Here be monsters

Then I heard a loud voice from the temple telling the seven angels, 'God and pour out on the earth the seven bowls of the wrath of God'... The sixth angel poured his bowl on the great River Euphrates, and its water was dried up in order to prepare the way for the kings from the east. And I saw three foul spirits like frogs coming from the mouth of the dragon, from the mouth of the beast, and from the mouth of the false prophet... And the demonic spirits assembled the kings at the place that in Hebrew is called Harmagedon.

The Exodus connection continues with seven plagues unleashed upon the earth, not unlike the ten plagues unleashed upon Egypt by Moses (see Exodus 7:14—12:32). The descriptions of contaminated water, scorching heat and (the sixth plague) the 'great River Euphrates' drying up bring to mind ongoing news stories about the climate emergency. Because of humanity's greed and irresponsibility, eco-disasters are now horribly commonplace, but frequency does not in any way lessen the suffering caused.

The Euphrates and Tigris rivers defined Mesopotamia (which means, literally, 'between rivers'), the land that was a cradle of early civilisation. In John's vision of disaster, the disappearance of the Euphrates opens the way for invasion 'from the east', the direction from which war so often came for ancient Israel. The dragon appears again, spouting hideous 'spirits like frogs', emblematic of the lies and distortions of truth associated with the beast and false prophet.

As in the days of Exodus, everything was going from bad to worse and the prospect of deliverance seemed remote. Meanwhile the forces of violence, oppression and deceit gather at a place which (in Greek) is known as Armageddon. The real-life Megiddo was a strategically important town in northern Israel, the site of a number of battles. Its appearance in Revelation has made it a name that has come to mean total annihilation.

'I am convinced that nothing can ever separate us from God's love. Neither death nor life, neither angels nor demons, neither our fears for today nor our worries about tomorrow – not even the powers of hell can separate us from God's love' (Romans 8:38, NLT).

NAOMI STARKEY

Unmaking

The seventh angel poured his bowl into the air, and a loud voice came out of the temple, from the throne, saying, 'It is done!' And there came flashes of lightning, rumblings, peals of thunder, and a violent earthquake, such as had not occurred since people were upon the earth, so violent was that earthquake. The great city was split into three parts, and the cities of the nations fell. God remembered great Babylon and gave her the wine cup of the fury of his wrath. And every island fled away, and no mountains were to be found; and huge hailstones… dropped from heaven.

The unmaking of the earth happens in a cataclysm as great as any 'Big Bang'. Maybe you remember the African American traditional spiritual song 'O sinner man, where you gonna run to?' with its scary lines about begging the rocks for a hiding place while the sea is 'a-boiling'. When the seventh bowl is poured, the planet is torn apart and all escape routes disappear.

The fearful prospect of judgement day begs the question: what kind of God would want these things to happen? As always, God's judgement needs to be held in tension with God's mercy – and individual passages to be read in the light of scripture as a whole. We should also remember that Revelation uses the bold language of apocalyptic. Today's reading is not a dire weather forecast for some fixed date in the future; it expresses the belief that God's purposes will prevail and all efforts to buy privileged exemption will fail.

The voice calling 'It is done!' points us back to the cross as the hinge of history. As he paid in full the price of sin, Jesus himself cried, 'It is finished' (John 19:30). The gospels describe unnatural darkness, earthquake and even the dead walking when the Son of God dies. The story of Easter reminds us, though, that God can bring new life (eternal life) out of the worst suffering, the greatest catastrophe. Remembering that will help guide us through the tumults of Revelation.

'Seek the Lord while he may be found… let the wicked forsake their way… let them return to the Lord, that he may have mercy on them' (Isaiah 55:6–7).

NAOMI STARKEY

Luxury and abomination

I saw a woman sitting on a scarlet beast that was full of blasphemous names... The woman was clothed in purple and scarlet and adorned with gold and jewels and pearls, holding in her hand a golden cup full of abominations and the impurities of her prostitution, and on her forehead was written a name, a mystery: 'Babylon the great, mother of whores and of earth's abominations.' And I saw that the woman was drunk with the blood of the saints and the blood of the witnesses to Jesus.

The book of Revelation is nothing if not full of energy, and here the energy spills over in rage. This woman is dazzling ('purple and scarlet' implying the very finest garments) and laden with jewellery, but her beauty is utterly corrupted by her behaviour. More than that, she is drunk 'with the blood of the saints', a dreadful, vampiric image.

Biblical writers often used prostitution and adultery as a metaphor for idolatry: the deliberate rejection of the Lord Almighty in favour of worshipping other lesser 'gods'. The dazzling, degenerate woman seated on the beast is identified as Babylon, capital of the empire that destroyed the Jerusalem temple and took God's people into exile. It is used here to symbolise the worst excesses of civilisation, so often found in concentrated form in cities. The most wretched poverty co-exists with the most decadent wealth, even sharing the same street, and scripture reminds us repeatedly that injustice and inequality are deeply abhorrent to God. Behind Babylon lurks the shadow of Babel, the tower (see Genesis 11) intended to mark the heights of human power in defiance of God's sovereign rule.

The rage in this vision makes for uncomfortable reading, especially as the central figure is a woman. We are rightly sensitive to the possibility of exploitation in such writing, rather than accepting it as showing flagrant wickedness. Having said that, this woman clothed in purple and scarlet is a counterpart to the woman 'clothed with the sun' (see 6 August), who gives birth to a saviour and triumphs over the dragon.

Pray for organisations such as Street Pastors,
who walk our cities to take care of the downfallen and downtrodden.

NAOMI STARKEY

Cracking the code

'This calls for a mind that has wisdom: the seven heads are seven mountains on which the woman is seated; also, they are seven kings, of whom five have fallen, one is living, and the other has not yet come, and when he comes, he must remain only a little while. As for the beast that was and is not, it is an eighth, but it belongs to the seven, and it goes to destruction. And the ten horns that you saw are ten kings who have not yet received a kingdom, but they are to receive authority as kings for one hour, together with the beast.'

These are dry and difficult verses, typical of the complexities of apocalyptic writing but without the strange glamour of dragons, beasts or bejewelled women. As the text itself points out, 'this calls for... wisdom'. Over the centuries, too much time and energy has been spent on wild speculation about this and other parts of Revelation. Wisdom may mean admitting that we cannot know for certain what the original author had in mind; a wise response can mean searching for wider principles in such passages, which can still guide us as we grow as disciples.

There are clues to help us find a wise reading. At a historical and practical level, Rome was built on seven hills, so the original audience of Revelation may well have identified that city and its associated empire – and its persecution of the church – with the realm of the beast or dragon. John's visions were a call to perseverance for believers living in a context of extraordinary challenge and danger. As the symbolism of 'seven' means a point or act of completion, so 'six' implies 'not yet'. As 21st-century followers of Jesus, we still live in the time of 'not yet': in the light of the resurrection while waiting for the final revelation of God's kingdom.

Christians are persecuted in many parts of the world, forced to meet in secret and forbidden to speak openly of their faith. Pray for God's blessing upon them and strength to protect them as they persevere in the 'not yet.'

NAOMI STARKEY

Being separate

Then I heard another voice from heaven saying, 'Come out of her, my people, so that you do not take part in her sins and so that you do not share in her plagues, for her sins are heaped high as heaven, and God has remembered her iniquities. Render to her as she herself has rendered, and repay her double for her deeds; mix a double dose for her in the cup she mixed. As she glorified herself and lived luxuriously, so give her a life measure of torment and grief. Since in her heart she says, "I rule as a queen; I am no widow, and I will never see grief", therefore her plagues will come in a single day.'

The call to 'come out of her, my people' has been used as a summons to separation throughout church history. Ideas and ideals of 'living together in love, with disagreement' have often foundered on the longing for purity, for clearer boundaries, and for more precise definitions of 'us' and 'them' (with 'us' clearly in the right). Context is always important, however, and the context here is not a call to Christians to separate from a corrupted church. It is more challenging: to live as salt and light in the world (see Matthew 5:13–14) without being distorted by the selfish values of Babylon.

The Babylon perspective is more than selfish; it denies reality, ignoring how actions have consequences and it maintains a permanent attitude of 'purchase now, pay never'. In contrast, the message of Revelation is that whatever is sown will be reaped; a merciless, predatory society will eventually consume itself.

As kingdom people, we have to live out a different way (which may cost us dearly) and show that God's heart is always for the last and least rather than those with the loudest voices and biggest bank accounts. In this act of witness, our ability to walk with fellow-believers with whom we disagree will speak more loudly and persuasively than any separatist neo-puritan agenda.

Jesus prayed that his disciples (including all those yet to come) 'may all be one' (John 17:21). How can the church today live out that prayer more fully?

NAOMI STARKEY

123

Downfall

The kings of the earth… will weep and wail over her when they see the smoke of her burning; they will… say, 'Alas, alas, the great city, Babylon, the mighty city! For in one hour your judgement has come.' And the merchants of the earth weep and mourn for her, since no one buys their cargo any more, cargo of gold, silver, jewels and pearls, fine linen, purple, silk and scarlet, all kinds of scented wood, all articles of ivory, all articles of costly wood, bronze, iron, and marble, cinnamon, spice, incense, myrrh, frankincense, wine, olive oil, choice flour and wheat, cattle and sheep, horses and chariots, slaves – and human lives.

The downfall of Babylon means the collapse of an entire economic system, something as shocking now as then, with 21st-century trade truly touching every part of the globe. The list of fine goods conjures up a bustling marketplace, dazzling with luxury, but at the end we find the shocking reminder that this economic system was built on slavery, at a terrible cost in human lives. In recent years, more and more countries have been acknowledging how their historic wealth was gained through exploitative trade practices and, above all, through slavery. This kind of honesty, accompanied by apology and appropriate reparations, can go some way towards making good (or at least making a bit better) the injustices of the past.

Sadly, if economic collapse ends the trade in human lives, it also brings universal hardship and calamity. Much that is beautiful and good is destroyed alongside the corrupted and bad; the innocent suffer as much as the guilty. As we saw yesterday, our response to Babylon should not be fleeing the complexities and compromises of the great city. Instead, we must be prepared to carry the light of God's kingdom into the very heart of the Babylon darkness. And we can do this without fear because we belong to the light and to the risen Lamb, who has triumphed over every beast and every dragon.

'But now thus says the Lord… Do not fear, for I have redeemed you;
I have called you by name, you are mine' (Isaiah 43:1).

NAOMI STARKEY

Psalms 52—66

 Over the next fortnight, we are spending time reflecting on excerpts from 15 of the psalms. The psalms in the Hebrew Bible are the hymnbook of the people of God, the place where the ups and downs of life are reflected upon and recorded. It is often said of the psalms that 'all life is here', meaning that they reflect the full range of human experiences and emotions. In our reflections, we shall encounter fear, anger and desperation, as well as trust, joy and praise. Many of the psalms we are reflecting upon are laments written when the people of God were under attack and in great danger. We shall see how they learn to lean on God, trusting in God to rescue and deliver them from their enemies. We shall see too how God remains steadfast throughout, faithful to the covenant of love made with the people of Israel. Towards the end of our fortnight, we will read some great hymns of praise in which all creation gives thanks for God's love and faithfulness.

From time to time, we shall also see how themes within the psalms are reflected in the life of Jesus. The psalms were Jesus' songbook and he knew them intimately, as did his first disciples. We will see how particular verses in the psalms resonate with the gospels and point to Jesus as the word of God made human: one with us, and for us.

The psalms encourage us to be real with God – to not be scared to come into God's presence and say how we are really feeling. Sometimes we think we have to be on our best behaviour with God, showing deference and being polite in God's presence. But God knows us through and through, so we can be confident to be really honest about how life is for us at any given time. It is just as important to complain to God about the difficult situations we find ourselves in as it is to be grateful when life is going well. With God, we can tell it how it really is, just as we would with a very close relative or friend. By turning to God in all circumstances we build a deep, trusting and loving relationship that will keep us secure and enable us to flourish in our faith.

CATHERINE WILLIAMS

Green olive tree

All day long you are plotting destruction. Your tongue is like a sharp razor, you worker of treachery. You love evil more than good and lying more than speaking the truth… But I am like a green olive tree in the house of God. I trust in the steadfast love of God forever and ever. I will thank you forever because of what you have done. In the presence of the faithful I will proclaim your name, for it is good.

Today's psalm contrasts a person of might and power bent on destruction with the faithful follower of God whose sense of purpose comes from trusting in God's steadfast love. The difference is stark and arresting.

The introduction to this psalm indicates that the tyrant is Doeg the Edomite, who slaughtered the priests of Nob when David visited Ahimelech (1 Samuel 21—22). Here is someone who chooses evil over good, rising to fame and fortune through destruction and deceit. Power and wealth have become his gods. The psalmist is confident that God will search him out, judging his rule of terror.

In contrast, the faithful person is portrayed as a green olive tree planted in God's house. The green olive tree is a potent symbol for God's people. Olive trees are a staple in the economy of the Holy Land. Olives are used daily for food, fuel, medicine and cosmetics, and also for holy rituals, such as anointing. Olive wood makes furniture, household goods and ornaments. Both prolific and durable, a healthy olive tree will produce abundantly for years. Virtually indestructible, olive trees can be ancient.

In the Hebrew scriptures, the olive tree stands for peace, fruitfulness and long life. The psalmist uses this symbol to describe the faithful follower of God. Such a follower readily expresses gratitude for all that God has done in the past, is doing now and will do in the future, telling others that God is good, loving and to be trusted. In what ways are you like God's green olive tree today?

Faithful God, may I be like a green olive tree: secure, useful, fruitful and holy. Help me to trust in your steadfast love forever. Amen.

CATHERINE WILLIAMS

Rejoice, be glad

Fools say in their hearts, 'There is no God.' They are corrupt; they commit abominable acts; there is no one who does good. God looks down from heaven on humankind to see if there are any who are wise, who seek after God. They have all fallen away; they are all alike perverse; there is no one who does good, no, not one... When God restores the fortunes of his people, Jacob will rejoice; Israel will be glad.

I was once at a school prizegiving ceremony, where the preacher – an invited guest – took the first verse of Psalm 53 as their text. The preacher declared to a large church full of young people, staff and parents that anyone who did not believe in God was a fool and an idiot. The preacher pronounced that such people were corrupt and capable only of wicked and sinful acts. We heard in no uncertain terms that unless we turned to God, we would be eternally damned. I listened in horrified astonishment. As you might imagine those assembled were angry and offended. The people of faith were embarrassed, as all were subjected to a harsh and belittling message, lacking the compassion, mercy and kindness of God, who gave himself for the entire world in Jesus. Such is the danger of taking verses out of context.

In Psalm 53 the psalmist is looking at his own people, the people of God and recognising some of the dangers of falling away, becoming lukewarm in faith or not maturing in holiness. Sometimes we hold to an immature view of the divine. Instead of being open to God's new and surprising ways, we expect God to act in the ways that seem best to us. It is all too easy to make God too small or in our own image. The good news is that God is always seeking us out, taking the initiative and enabling us to grow deeper in faith and divine intimacy. God will not let us go. Nothing we do can stop God loving us. God comes to us in Jesus, this is how our fortunes are restored, and so there is much in which to rejoice and be glad.

Thank you for loving me just as I am.
Enable my love for you to keep maturing. Amen.

CATHERINE WILLIAMS

Argh! Help me!

Save me, O God, by your name, and vindicate me by your might. Hear my prayer, O God; give ear to the words of my mouth. For the insolent have risen against me; the ruthless seek after my life; they do not set God before them… My heart is in anguish within me; the terrors of death have fallen upon me… But I call upon God, and the Lord will save me… Cast your burden on the Lord, and he will sustain you.

Many years ago on a retreat, the wise priest leading said that there are two prayers every Christian should know by heart and be prepared to use. The first is 'Argh!' – a cry of strong emotion – followed swiftly by the second: 'Help me!'

This type of praying is ably demonstrated in Psalms 54 and 55. The psalmist cries out to God, calls for help and implores God to act. Under attack, the psalmist turns to God trusting that God will rescue and restore. The psalmist also asks God to deal with those who are attacking him. In recognition of God's intervention, the psalmist gives thanks, makes an offering and speaks God's name to others.

As a spiritual director, I listen to complex and troubling situations that affect others. I encourage people to cry out to God, express their deepest feelings and ask God for help and protection. The ways that such prayers are answered can be astonishing and very humbling. Together we find ourselves giving thanks to God and discussing the brilliant ways God solves the seemingly impossible. Sometimes this happens very quickly; other times it takes many years of faithful prayer and trust. This may also include following Jesus' injunction to pray for those who cause us trouble (Matthew 5:44) and believing that God will bring new life from deadly situations – just as in Jesus, whose life we share.

If you are currently going through difficulties, cry out to God: 'Argh!' Call on God: 'Help me!' Trust that God will act for good. Patience and openness to God's timing and ways are key. And when you realise that God has acted and brought new life, give thanks and tell others.

Lord, remind me to cry out to you for help when times are tough. Amen.

CATHERINE WILLIAMS

God knows

You have kept count of my tossings; put my tears in your bottle. Are they not in your record? Then my enemies will retreat in the day when I call. This I know, that God is for me. In God, whose word I praise, in the Lord, whose word I praise, in God I trust; I am not afraid. What can a mere mortal do to me?

The themes of fear and trust are woven throughout Psalm 56. As with the psalms we explored yesterday, the psalmist, under attack, is crying out to God. Oppressed by those who fight and trample, lurk and stir up strife, the psalmist feels the attack is relentless. Perhaps you have been in situations that feel like this. Perhaps you are in such a situation now. At such times, deep fear in the core of our being can take hold. But the psalmist is determined not to let such fear have the upper hand. Perspective is gained by turning to God and trusting deeply in God's promise to rescue and save. People can cause great damage, but they are only flesh and blood. In contrast, God is almighty, eternal and loving.

This is the God who keeps track of all our comings and goings – who is with us on every journey: physical, emotional and spiritual. 'Wanderings' is a better translation than 'tossings' in verse 8. This is the God who knows us through and through and notices everything that happens to us. God is so involved in our lives that even our tears are kept, held safely and preserved. Various cultures from the ancient Greeks and Romans to the more recent Victorians kept the tears of their deceased loved ones in special bottles called lachrymatory phials or tear-catchers. It is a beautiful thought: God holding and cherishing all our tears – of sorrow and joy, mourning and celebration.

Staying close to God, and dwelling in God's word enables trust and faith to blossom, sufficient to overcome fear. For the Christian God's word became incarnate in Jesus, the one who overcame not only fear but also death, opening the way to new life for all.

Lord God, thank you that you know and notice everything about me.
When I am afraid help me to trust in you. Amen

CATHERINE WILLIAMS

A steadfast heart

Be merciful to me, O God; be merciful to me, for in you my soul takes refuge; in the shadow of your wings I will take refuge, until the destroying storms pass by… I lie down among lions that greedily devour human prey; their teeth are spears and arrows, their tongues sharp swords… My heart is steadfast, O God; my heart is steadfast… Be exalted, O God, above the heavens. Let your glory be over all the earth.

John Lennon is credited with saying: 'Everything will be okay in the end. If it's not okay, it's not the end.' Psalm 57 encapsulates this wise thought. The psalmist continues to be under attack. The enemies are like beasts of prey, who bite and tear. Their words are destructive weapons – attacking at a deep level. Our psalmist is surrounded by storms and devastation. This is a very present reality. Perhaps it is a reality for you too.

But there is another reality to hold on to – that of a loving and faithful God who has rescued before and can be relied on to do so again. The shadow of God's wings is a place of safety and refuge. This beautiful maternal image is one picked up by Jesus, who likens himself to a mother hen longing to gather and protect her chicks (Luke 13:34). It is also reminiscent of the Spirit, who broods over the waters at the beginning of creation (Genesis 1:2), waiting to breathe new life into emptiness.

The psalmist responds with joy to this protective and nurturing care. The future is secure, and this assurance enables praise and thanksgiving to bubble over. Our psalmist's desire to sing for joy is sufficient to call a new day into life. When our hearts can hold and reflect God's steadfast love and faithfulness, even in the middle of devastation, then hope is possible: 'Everything will be okay in the end. If it's not okay, it's not the end.' God is in everything, through everything and over everything. Therefore, we can have confidence and hope even when times are tough, the journey long and hard or we can't see a way forward. In the end, everything will be okay.

Lord, make my heart steadfast, even in the toughest times. Amen.

CATHERINE WILLIAMS

Really angry!

The wicked go astray from the womb… They have venom like the venom of a serpent, like the deaf adder that stops its ear, so that it does not hear the voice of charmers… O God, break the teeth in their mouths; tear out the fangs of the young lions, O Lord! Let them vanish like water that runs away; like grass let them be trodden down and wither. Let them be like the snail that dissolves into slime.

What makes you angry? Really angry! Is it a person, a group of people or a situation in your community or in the world today? Think for a moment and identify an injustice that really makes your blood boil. Sometimes only a full-on rant will do. Jesus knew that: overturning the money changers' tables in the temple (Matthew 21:12) or calling the religious authorities a 'brood of vipers' (Matthew 12:34).

Today our psalmist is uncompromisingly angry. Psalm 58 is an uncomfortable psalm, with its intense, violent language and vicious imagery. We might feel embarrassed to read out this psalm in public worship. The writer is absolutely furious and in desperation pours out anger and bitterness. The evil of the community leaders is exposed. They are like snakes who are both poisonous and deaf. Unable to hear the voice of the snake charmer, they cannot be controlled.

It gives a powerful image of chaos unleashed where violence and wickedness have the upper hand. The psalmist calls out for God to intervene and suggests ways that these leaders might be stopped – from disarming them to making them dissolve or vanish. The psalmist looks forward to a time when the wicked will be judged and the righteous will celebrate and rejoice in a God who overturns injustice here and now.

Back to the person, people or situation that is making you angry. What would you like to say to God about that? How would you like God to act? Tell God about it now, and in the privacy of your own home, do not be afraid to strongly express how you are feeling deep down inside.

'Hear my prayer, O Lord; let my cry come to you' (Psalm 102:1). Amen.

CATHERINE WILLIAMS

Night and day

Each evening they come back, howling like dogs and prowling about the city. They roam about for food and growl if they do not get their fill. But I will sing of your might; I will sing aloud of your steadfast love in the morning. For you have been a fortress for me and a refuge in the day of my distress. O my strength, I will sing praises to you, for you, O God, are my fortress, the God who shows me steadfast love.

It is well-known that dangers seem worse at night, in the dark. When we are anxious, we find it hard to sleep, and our worries seem greater as we lie awake in silence. Aches and pains, fevers and illnesses often seem worse in the small hours. Many parents will have experienced anxious trips to hospitals with young children in the middle of the night. The Samaritans receive their highest volume of calls from people in suicidal crisis during the very early hours of the morning. The empty space of night awakens our imaginations, and suddenly things that are very unlikely to happen – burglary, fire or worse – are just a heartbeat away.

In Psalm 59 our psalmist is again calling for protection and deliverance from those who are making life intolerable through their evil acts. The psalmist likens them to wild dogs who roam the city at night, howling and baying for blood, looking for anything or anyone they can attack and eat. Such terrors of the night are overwhelming. The psalmist calls on God to wake up and help. To be a strong safe place, a fortress and a refuge, where the enemy is barred from entry.

To quell these night-time fears, the psalmist commits to singing confidently in the morning – telling all the world of God's faithful and steadfast love. Starting each day by recalling God's love is such a good plan. Reminding ourselves that God will be with us, whatever happens, is easier at the beginning of the day when we often feel more secure. What is your favourite hymn or song about God's love? Why not sing or listen to it now?

Lord, hold me secure in the darkness. Teach me to sing in the light. Amen.

CATHERINE WILLIAMS

God is with us

O God, you have rejected us, broken our defences; you have been angry; now restore us! You have caused the land to quake; you have torn it open; repair the cracks in it, for it is tottering... Give victory with your right hand and answer us, so that those whom you love may be rescued. God has promised in his sanctuary, 'With exultation I will divide up Shechem and portion out the Vale of Succoth.'

Psalm 60 is a national lament following a series of military defeats for the people of Israel. Through the psalmist, the people cry out to God, articulating their confusion and desperation. It appears that God has rejected them, causing their world to come tumbling down. While the people endure such suffering, it seems that God's promises are not being fulfilled. They call out for help and long to be rescued. A vivid picture is painted of the people's desperate situation. Emotions are raw. God takes them back to the original promise made when they entered the land. All the areas of the land belong to God who portions them out, working for the good of the people. God is with them.

It is not always possible to understand what God is doing. Sometimes God seems to be absent, unengaged or deliberately working against what seems good. At such times we might be confused, angry or despairing with God. We might doubt God's existence or find a seeming lack of care or interest hard to defend. It is important to remember that God is *God*: vast, eternal and so much bigger than our ability to comprehend. God is at work on the entire cosmic canvas, not just our tiny corner of it. God's ways are not our ways. We see that clearly in Jesus, fully God and fully human, whose birth, life, death and resurrection point to mysteries far deeper than we can imagine. When our world is turned upside down, and we are confused, angry or desperate, questioning God is part of the journey that leads to the rekindling of trust and faith. God is with us through everything, working ultimately for good.

Let us pray with Julian of Norwich: 'All shall be well, and all shall be well, and all manner of things shall be well.' Amen.

CATHERINE WILLIAMS

Freedom and safety

Hear my cry, O God; listen to my prayer. From the end of the earth I call to you, when my heart is faint. Lead me to the rock that is higher than I, for you are my refuge, a strong tower against the enemy. Let me abide in your tent forever, find refuge under the shelter of your wings... So I will always sing praises to your name, as I pay my vows day after day.

Following the traumatic events of World War II, the United Nations was established to foster international peace. In 1948 representatives from the 50 member states met under the guidance of Eleanor Roosevelt to devise a list of human rights. From this, the Universal Declaration of Human Rights was proclaimed. Article 3 asserts: 'Everyone has the right to life, liberty and security of person.'

Our psalmist today is crying out to God for this right. From a place of separation, on the margins ('the end of the earth') and feeling powerless and vulnerable ('a faint heart'), the psalmist turns to God for safety and security. Note of all those words for such a place: rock, refuge, strong tower, tent, shelter. We all need a place in which to feel safe and secure – it is now recognised as a basic human right. For our desire – like the psalmist's – is to be with God.

We are made to be with God. Augustine of Hippo famously wrote in his *Confessions*: 'Our hearts are restless until they find their rest in you.' We long to be where God is, to share God's tent, to be held secure under God's wings. Here again is that comforting maternal image that we explored in Psalm 57. This sense of safety and security leads the psalmist to praise God and commit to remaining obedient and faithful.

As Christians, our security comes from another of those words: 'rock'. Jesus, the stone which the builders rejected, is the chief cornerstone, the one on which our faith is built. And we are living stones, incorporated into Jesus the rock through our baptism. Jesus is our security, our place of freedom and safety.

'Rock of ages, cleft for me, let me hide myself in thee'
(Augustus Toplady, 1740–78). Amen.

CATHERINE WILLIAMS

Waiting in silence

For God alone my soul waits in silence; from him comes my salvation… For God alone my soul waits in silence, for my hope is from him. He alone is my rock and my salvation, my fortress; I shall not be shaken. On God rests my deliverance and my honour; my mighty rock, my refuge is in God. Trust in him at all times, O people; pour out your heart before him; God is a refuge for us.

In Psalm 62 the deafening assaults of the enemy are contrasted with the stillness of the faithful soul waiting on God. This silence and stillness seem to speak deeply to us, drawing us in. Over the past week, the psalmists have cried out to God, called for help and sung praises when rescue came. Today's psalmist waits in silence – entering into the still centre of God's fathomless love.

Western culture is fast and frenetic. It is hard to sit in silence and wait. We expect immediate results, and many get stressed and anxious when not in control of events. Our world is busy and noisy. Technology has made sound constant in our society, whether it be computers, smartphones, recorded music, television or traffic. For many, there is rarely silence, and when it is encountered it can be unsettling and deeply alien.

A while back, I undertook a 30-day silent retreat at a religious house. During nearly five weeks of silence, I spoke only once a day to my spiritual guide, took Holy Communion and read set passages of scripture. I was discouraged from reading other books, listening to music, using technology or contacting anyone. At first, the experience was bewildering and the time stretched endlessly. Entering deeply into silence, my head cleared, my body relaxed and I rediscovered the profound love of God for me, the love I have always known deep inside but which had been shouted down by the busy, noisy world. This reconnection with God has been life-changing.

You may already know the benefits of sitting in silence and waiting on God. If it is not something you have encountered, I encourage you to take time to sit still, in complete silence and allow yourself to be overwhelmed by God's eternal love.

Lord, help me to embrace you in stillness and silence. Amen.

CATHERINE WILLIAMS

135

God: present and personal

O God, you are my God; I seek you; my soul thirsts for you; my flesh faints for you, as in a dry and weary land where there is no water. So I have looked upon you in the sanctuary, beholding your power and glory. Because your steadfast love is better than life, my lips will praise you. So I will bless you as long as I live; I will lift up my hands and call on your name.

The preface to today's psalm indicates that it reflects the time when King David was in the wilderness of Judah escaping his enemies (1 Samuel 22—26). In this dry, barren and inhospitable place, the king yearns to feel God's presence. He likens it to longing for water to revive his thirst. He desperately seeks the sustaining and life-giving relationship that comes from intimacy with the one he calls 'my God'. In order to experience God with him, David recalls the presence of God in the temple. This reminds him that God's love is steadfast. This is sufficient to turn his thirsty lips to praise. His fainting flesh now stands tall, with hands lifted high. God is not only to be found in the temple but in the wilderness too. God is present with David. The relationship is deep and personal.

How is your soul today? Are you feeling close to God and well-watered or is your faith going through a dry patch? Perhaps you are in something of a spiritual desert. Our faith forebears went through wilderness times too. Not only David, but the Israelites as they came out of Egypt and Jesus too as he began his ministry. At such times we learn to seek God in unexpected places and new ways.

As Christians, we experience God with us in Jesus, and this personal relationship can help us become more aware of the God who is to be found not just in church, but beside us through all of life. Jesus is a continuous spring of living water (John 4:14) that quenches our spiritual thirst and leads us to new life.

Lord, when the desert encroaches and our wells have run dry,
lead us back to you, our living water. Amen.

CATHERINE WILLIAMS

The words of my mouth

Hide me from the secret plots of the wicked, from the scheming of evil-doers, who whet their tongues like swords, who aim bitter words like arrows, shooting from ambush at the blameless; they shoot suddenly and without fear... But God will shoot his arrow at them; they will be wounded suddenly. Because of their tongue he will bring them to ruin... Let the righteous rejoice in the Lord and take refuge in him. Let all the upright in heart glory.

If you have ever been on the receiving end of a vicious verbal attack or ongoing chronic verbal abuse, you will know how painful and damaging words can be. I have often thought that the traditional saying 'Sticks and stones may break my bones, but words can never hurt me' is not strictly true. While words may not cause physical pain, they can cause huge emotional and psychological damage, both in the moment and for many years after. Words have the ability to lodge themselves deep within us and shape our self-image, our thoughts and our actions.

In Psalm 64, the psalmist experiences the bitter words of enemies as an attack with weapons: 'tongues like swords' and 'words like arrows'. In such a scenario, it is all too easy to retaliate with strong and vicious words ourselves, either in direct response to our attacker or by seeking to undermine them by spreading gossip and lies behind their back.

The psalmist does not retaliate but calls on God to bring about justice, expressing the hope that the words of the attackers will be their downfall. The psalmist looks to God as a place of safety where the heart can rejoice.

In the letter of James, we are warned that the tongue is a powerful tool, which can be used both to curse and to bless (3:1–10). Take a moment now to think about the words you have spoken recently. Have they been damaging and destructive words or words of life and blessing? How can you choose your words so that they build up and bless others?

'Let the words of my mouth, and the meditation of my heart,
be acceptable in thy sight, O Lord, my strength, and my redeemer'
(Psalm 19:14, KJV). Amen.

CATHERINE WILLIAMS

Creation's praise

By awesome deeds you answer us with deliverance, O God of our salvation; you are the hope of all the ends of the earth and of the farthest seas. By your strength you established the mountains; you are girded with might. You silence the roaring of the seas, the roaring of their waves, the tumult of the peoples. Those who live at earth's farthest bounds are awed by your signs; you make the gateways of the morning and the evening shout for joy.

After many psalms of lament and distress, today's psalm is a great hymn of praise. Probably sung as part of a festival to celebrate the year's cycle of growth, Psalm 65 is directed to God, who is both the Lord of creation and the Lord of forgiveness. The people have come to God's holy place to be cleansed, forgiven and renewed. They recall God's incredible deeds and renew their faith and hope in the one who is over, in and through all creation. God is Lord of the entire created order, which praises God through its fruitfulness, abundance and beauty.

Who is not awed by a spectacular sunrise or sunset? For the psalmist, such a sight is the beginning and end of each day shouting for joy to its creator. This passionate image reminds us that everything God has made bears witness to God's glory and is under divine care and protection.

One of the ways we see God revealed in Jesus is through miracles which break the laws of nature. Jesus heals those born blind, multiplies loaves and fishes and raises the dead. After the stilling of the storm on Lake Galilee, the disciples ask: 'Who then is this, that he commands even the winds and the water and they obey him?' (Luke 8:25). Can you see the link with Psalm 65? It is God who silences the 'roaring of the seas', and this 'awesome deed' is replicated by God in Jesus, whom the waves obey.

Next time you are outdoors, try to notice the ways in which the created order is praising the Lord. How does your life bear witness to the life-giving presence of God?

Lord, help me to praise you with every fibre of my being! Amen.

CATHERINE WILLIAMS

Recalling God's deeds

Come and see what God has done: he is awesome in his deeds among mortals… Bless our God, O peoples; let the sound of his praise be heard, who has kept us among the living and has not let our foot slip… Come and hear, all you who fear God, and I will tell you what he has done for me… Blessed be God, who has not rejected my prayer or removed his steadfast love from me.

Our final psalm in these reflections is another great hymn of praise. Psalm 66 recalls the ways in which God has rescued and saved both the community and the psalmist personally. Through times of trial and testing God has remained faithful to the people, and in return they bring offerings and thanksgiving to God. Past and present come together as the historic deliverance of the Israelites from Egypt is recalled and the psalmist praises God's consistent presence and support.

When times are tough, or we are struggling with life or faith, it can be a good practice to think back to a time when we have been very aware of God with us and celebrate that again. Recalling God's good actions towards us in the past makes them a present reality and can help us trust God to act for good again. This is true both for the Christian community as a whole and for each of us as individual disciples. Some Christians keep a journal where they record their faith experiences. Looking back through past entries is a helpful reminder of God's love and goodness. If this is not something you have done, you might like to try it.

Sharing with one another what God has done enables all of us to be inspired and to grow in faith. 'Come and see… come and hear…' says the psalmist, who is longing to tell everyone about God's amazing love and faithfulness.

Where have you seen God act for good, either in your faith community or in your own life? What are you longing to tell others about God? Ask the Holy Spirit to bring to mind someone to whom you can tell your experiences.

Thank you, Lord, for all I have learned of you
during these recent reflections on the psalms. Amen.

CATHERINE WILLIAMS

If you've enjoyed the reflections
by **Michael Mitton** and **David Walker**,
check out their books published with BRF, including…

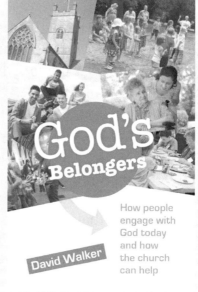

Seasoned by Seasons
Flourishing in life's experiences

God's Belongers
*How people engage with God
today and how the church can help*

978 0 85746 540 5
£7.99

978 0 85746 467 5
£7.99

To order, visit **brfonline.org.uk** or use the order form at the end.

Living Faith

I would like to make a donation to support BRF Ministries.
Please use my gift for:

☐ Where the need is greatest ☐ Anna Chaplaincy ☐ Living Faith

☐ Messy Church ☐ Parenting for Faith

Title   First name/initials   Surname

Address

Postcode

Email

Telephone

Signature   Date

Our ministry is only possible because of the generous support of individuals, churches, trusts and gifts in wills.

Please treat as Gift Aid donations all qualifying gifts of money made (*tick all that apply*)

giftaid it

☐ today, ☐ in the past four years, ☐ and in the future.

I am a UK taxpayer and understand that if I pay less Income Tax and/or Capital Gains Tax in the current tax year than the amount of Gift Aid claimed on all my donations, it is my responsibility to pay any difference.

☐ My donation does not qualify for Gift Aid.

Please notify us if you want to cancel this Gift Aid declaration, change your name or home address, or no longer pay sufficient tax on your income and/or capital gains.

You can also give online at **brf.org.uk/donate**, which reduces our administration costs, making your donation go further.

Please complete other side of form ➲

141

SHARING OUR VISION – MAKING A GIFT

Please accept my gift of:

☐ £2 ☐ £5 ☐ £10 ☐ £20 Other £ ▢

by (*delete as appropriate*):

☐ Cheque/Charity Voucher payable to 'BRF'

☐ MasterCard/Visa/Debit card/Charity card

Name on card

Card no. ☐☐☐☐ ☐☐☐☐ ☐☐☐☐ ☐☐☐☐

Expires end ☐☐☐☐   Security code* ☐☐☐   *Last 3 digits on the reverse of the card

Signature   Date

☐ I would like to leave a gift to BRF Ministries in my will.
  Please send me further information.

☐ I would like to find out about giving a regular gift to BRF Ministries.

For help or advice regarding making a gift, please contact our fundraising team **+44 (0)1865 462305**

Your privacy

We will use your personal data to process this transaction. From time to time we may send you information about the work of BRF Ministries that we think may be of interest to you. Our privacy policy is available at **brf.org.uk/privacy**. Please contact us if you wish to discuss your mailing preferences.

Registered with

FUNDRAISING
REGULATOR

 Please complete other side of form

Please return this form to 'Freepost BRF'
No other address information or stamp is needed

Bible Reading Fellowship is a charity (233280) and company limited by guarantee (301324), registered in England and Wales

Reading New Daylight in a group

GORDON GILES

It is good to talk. While the Rule of Benedict, which formed the spiritual foundations of the daily prayer life of so many ecclesiastical foundations, recommended daily scripture reading as a key aspect of the community life of work and prayer, discussion and reflection are a good consequence of reading passages that others are reading simultaneously. Separated by space, as each reads alone, we are yet connected by the common food of scripture, taken in our own time at our own pace. We each chew on it in our own way. Yet discussion or shared reflection on the passages chosen and the comments made can aid digestion, so here are some 'open' questions that may enable discussion in a Bible study or other group who gather to take further what is published here. The same questions may also aid personal devotion. Use them as you wish, and may God bless and inspire you on your journey as you read, mark and inwardly digest holy words to ponder and nourish the soul.

General discussion starters

These can be used for any study series within this issue. Remember there are no right or wrong answers – these questions are simply to enable a group to engage in conversation.

- What do you think is the main idea or theme of the author in this series? Did that come across strongly?

- Have any of the issues discussed touched on personal – or shared – aspects of your life?

- What evidence or stories do the authors draw on to illuminate or be illuminated by the passages of scripture?

- Which do you prefer: scripture informing daily modern life, or modern life shining a new light on scripture?

- Does the author 'call you to action' in a realistic and achievable way? Do you think their ideas will work in the secular world?

- Have any specific passages struck you personally? If so, how and why? Is God speaking to you through scripture and reflection?

- Was anything completely new to you? Any 'eureka' or jaw-dropping moments? If so, what difference will that make?

Questions for group discussion

Silence (David Walker)

- Is there enough silence in your pattern of prayer and worship, both individually and with others?
- Can you recall an occasion when you felt the presence or voice of God in silence? What happened in consequence?
- Was there a time when you broke a dangerous or destructive silence, or wish you had had the courage to do so?
- What is your experience of being present with someone who needs your silent accompaniment, not your words?
- Looking back, can you identify times when you have allowed other voices to drown the voice of God?

Romans 12—16 (Lakshmi Jeffreys)

- Why can it feel easier to offer our minds and seek to renew our bodies, rather than offering our bodies and asking God to renew our minds?
- How can we tell if we are conforming to the standards of the world? What can we do about it?
- What do you think and feel about national and international leaders and civic authorities?
- How might the Christian church practically and prayerfully support what is godly and challenge what is not?
- How do you manage differences of opinion in your church? What might Paul teach us through Romans?

Holy days and holidays (Louise Davis)

- Reflect together and share memories of holidays from your youth.
- Where is God in a holiday?
- What is the difference between a holiday and a pilgrimage?
- Think about the Bible passages chosen – can you think of any others that speak of holy days and holidays?
- How can we keep any day holy?
- Do we need holy days and holidays?

Psalms 52—66 (Catherine Williams)

- In what ways have you experienced God's steadfast love?

- There are many images used in these psalms to evoke safety and security (e.g. tower, rock, fortress, wings). Which image most resonates with you and why?

- How do you react to the angry and violent words used in some of these psalms?

- The psalmist regularly speaks of praising God. How do you express your gratitude to God?

- What roles do silence and stillness play in your prayer life?

- We have been exploring links between Jesus and the psalms – what further links can you find?

Meet the author: Martin Leckebusch

How did you come to faith?

I was raised in a family which was nominally Methodist and went regularly to the local Methodist Sunday School. However, it was not until I was taken to a Pentecostal church by a school friend during my teenage years that I made my own commitment to Christ.

How has your faith and your working life connected?

After studying mathematics at university, I spent 37 years in information technology, mostly for a major UK bank. The main direct impact of my faith there was the challenge of performing a technical job in a cost-conscious, time-pressured environment with integrity, helping colleagues with my skills and experience wherever I could.

What is your current ministry?

I was fortunate to be able to take retirement at Easter 2022, which has given me more time for writing. Besides that, I am on the leadership team at the Baptist church my wife and I attend in Gloucester, where we co-lead a home group and I also preach regularly.

What do you write?

My main writing over the past three decades has been hymn lyrics. I find this a fascinating and satisfying way to 'do theology', exploring issues of faith and responding to God's grace. I've had a number of hymns published, in various hymnals in the UK and the USA.

Who has inspired you in the Bible and why?

Barnabas intrigues me. He was willing to take unpopular and even risky decisions and, as a result, persuaded people to take Saul of Tarsus seriously and drew John Mark back into Christian service. That means we are probably indirectly indebted to Barnabas for a third of the New Testament!

Recommended reading

Jonathan Arnold, a seasoned community engagement expert, delves deep into the heart of the biblical mandate to love one's neighbour. Through a tapestry of real-life stories, he unveils the power of practical faith, illustrating how it can ignite transformation among the homeless, refugees, the poor and vulnerable, imprisoned and marginalised, as well as those living with dementia, disability and disease.

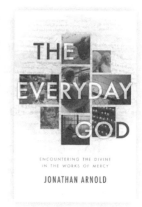

In these pages, you'll witness how acts of social and environmental justice, intertwined with mercy, have the potential to reshape lives, offering a vivid portrait of the profound impact of embracing the everyday God. As he reflects upon Jesus's teaching in Matthew 25:34–40, Arnold challenges us to discover God's presence in the most unexpected places and join in with where he is acting, whether inside or outside our churches.

The following is an edited extract taken from the Introduction.

To talk about an everyday God is to recognise that to live fully as a Christian is to see and hear where God is acting, whether inside or outside our churches, and to join in with that work. The music of our mission as Christians is to join in with the melody of the *missio Dei*, God's mission.

I am fortunate to work with a team of skilled and passionate people who manage projects aligned with the seven works of mercy. The Social Justice Network team is an outward-facing framework of the diocese that works to express our faith in God through involvement in high-profile topical issue areas such as prisons, homelessness, deprivation and forced migration. We build relationships with partner networks to discern and develop new audiences for future engagement.

Every day there are stories of healing and hope. This work has emerged as a testament to these initiatives, and in response to the many social and community projects within our parishes, villages and towns. Drawing upon this experience in community, I hope to explore how the biblical imperative to love one's neighbour through practical and applied faith is evident in the works of mercy found in Matthew 25:35–40 and in people today, and how these works of mercy are a means of grace, through which God gives blessing, forgiveness, life and salvation.

Through these true stories of everyday lives lived courageously and generously in the service of one another, *The Everyday God* shares observations of lives transformed through the dedication of ordinary people seeking to follow Christ, and thereby reflects upon Jesus' call to feed the hungry, clothe the naked (shelter the homeless), give drink to the thirsty, heal the sick, visit the imprisoned, welcome the stranger and bury the dead. Pope Francis added an extra spiritual work of mercy in 2016, to care for our environment, which will also be explored in this work.

By using the term 'everyday God' I am not referring to the idea that 'God is not just for Sunday' or '24/7 discipleship' or 'fresh expressions' of being church; nor am I centred on who we are and what we do as Christians. Rather, I am focused on who *God* is and *where* God is and *what* God is doing there. It is God's music, Christ's melody that is playing, and if we tune in and listen, we might be able to hear it, be moved by it, sing along with it. We might even find ourselves in harmony with it and with one another.

If there is an 'everyday God', then I guess there must also be an 'everyday theology'. So, what is it? Kevin Vanhoozer describes everyday theology as 'faith seeking understanding of everyday life. Nothing should be easier to understand than the notion of "the everyday" for the simple reason that it is so commonplace.' It is a curiosity, a seeking, a questioning born out of our faith. And hence we don't need any special place or institution to be an everyday theologian. Our laboratory is the everyday and the ordinary, whatever and wherever that might be for you, because God's grace is in the everyday.

God is revealed through the ordinary, because God is at the very heart of every human experience. Through the creation of the world, through the *Logos* (Christ), to the incarnation of Jesus, God has demonstrated that he dwells with us, as Paul Tillich put it, 'as the ground of our being'. This divine gift of grace at the depths of our human existence is Christ's identification with 'the least' (Matthew 25:40). We do not, therefore, treat our neighbour as a means to an end, a means to receiving or invoking divine grace, but rather that the everyday encounter is made holy. It follows that we love and serve our neighbour for their own sake, as they do for us, and in so doing forget our own selfish concerns. Only then can the encounter be grace-filled. The challenge that God's work in the world sets for us is how to tune into God's love, service, mercy and justice. How do we connect with the work of God? How do we join in with the music of God, and play his theme of mercy.

To order a copy of this book, please use the order form or visit **brfonline.org.uk**

Weaving together biblical perspectives with academic research and his own experiences of working in different settings, Chris Gillies lays the theological foundation for work, moves on to examining biblical role models from both Old and New Testaments, and concludes by exploring common issues we wrestle with in our work, from money matters or managing and leading others to knowing if we're in the right job or simply doing the right thing.

On the Way to Work
A Christian approach to thinking differently about success and fulfilment
Chris Gillies

978 1 80039 239 7 £12.99
brfonline.org.uk

To order

Delivery times within the UK are normally 15 working days. Prices are correct at the time of going to press but may change without prior notice.

Title	Price	Qty	Total
On the Way to Work	£12.99		
Seasoned by Seasons	£7.99		
God's Belongers	£7.99		
The Everyday God	£9.99		

POSTAGE AND PACKING CHARGES			
Order value	UK	Europe	Rest of world
Under £7.00	£2.00	Available on request	Available on request
£7.00–£29.99	£3.00		
£30.00 and over	FREE		

Total value of books	
Postage and packing	
Donation*	
Total for this order	

* Please complete and return the Gift Aid declaration on page 141.

Please complete in BLOCK CAPITALS

Title _____ First name/initials _____ Surname _____

Address _____

_____ Postcode _____

Acc. No. _____ Telephone _____

Email _____

Method of payment

☐ Cheque (made payable to BRF) ☐ MasterCard / Visa

Card no. ☐☐☐☐ ☐☐☐☐ ☐☐☐☐ ☐☐☐☐

Expires end ☐☐ ☐☐ Security code ☐☐☐ Last 3 digits on the reverse of the card

We will use your personal data to process this order. From time to time we may send you information about the work of BRF Ministries. Please contact us if you wish to discuss your mailing preferences. Our privacy policy is available at **brf.org.uk/privacy**.

Please return this form to:

BRF Ministries, 15 The Chambers, Vineyard, Abingdon OX14 3FE | **enquiries@brf.org.uk**
For terms and cancellation information, please visit **brfonline.org.uk/terms**.

Bible Reading Fellowship (BRF) is a charity (233280) and company limited by guarantee (301324), registered in England and Wales

BRF Ministries needs you!

If you're one of our many thousands of regular *New Daylight* readers you will know all about the benefits and blessings of regular Bible reading and the value of daily notes to guide, inform and inspire you. Here are some recent comments from *New Daylight* readers:

> 'Thank you for all the many inspiring writings that help so much when things are tough.'

> 'Just right for me – I learned a lot!'

> 'We looked forward to each day's message as we pondered each passage and comment.'

If you have similarly positive things to say about *New Daylight*, would you be willing to share your experience with others? Could you ask for a brief slot during church notices or write a short piece for your church magazine or website? Do you belong to groups, formal or informal, where you could share your experience of using Bible reading notes and encourage others to try them?

It doesn't need to be complicated or nerve-wracking: just answering these three questions in what you say or write will get your message across:

- How do Bible reading notes help you grow in your faith?
- Where, when and how do you use them?
- What would you say to people who don't already use them?

We can supply further information if you need it and would love to hear about it if you do give a talk or write an article.

For more information:

- Email **enquiries@brf.org.uk**
- Phone us on **+44 (0)1865 319700** Mon–Fri 9.30–17.00
- Write to us at BRF Ministries, 15 The Chambers, Vineyard, Abingdon OX14 3FE

Inspiring people of all ages to grow in Christian faith

At BRF Ministries, we long for people of all ages to grow in faith and understanding of the Bible. That's what all our work as a charity is about.

- Our **Living Faith** range of resources helps Christians go deeper in their understanding of scripture, in prayer and in their walk with God. Our conferences and events bring people together to share this journey, while our Holy Habits resources help whole congregations grow together as disciples of Jesus, living out and sharing their faith.

- We also want to make it easier for local churches to engage effectively in ministry and mission – by helping them bring new families into a growing relationship with God through **Messy Church** or by supporting churches as they nurture the spiritual life of older people through **Anna Chaplaincy**.

- Our **Parenting for Faith** team coaches parents and others to raise God-connected children and teens, and enables churches to fully support them.

Do you share our vision?

Though a significant proportion of BRF Ministries' funding is generated through our charitable activities, we are dependent on the generous support of individuals, churches and charitable trusts.

If you share our vision, would you help us to enable even more people of all ages to grow in faith? Your prayers and financial support are vital for the work that we do. You could:

- support us with a regular donation or one-off gift
- consider leaving a gift to BRF Ministries in your will
- encourage your church to support us as part of your church's giving to home mission – perhaps focusing on a specific ministry or programme
- most important of all, support us with your prayers.

Donate at **brf.org.uk/donate** or use the form on pages 141–42.

Bearing fruit

'Remain in me, as I also remain in you. No branch can bear fruit by itself; it must remain in the vine. Neither can you bear fruit unless you remain in me.'

JOHN 15:4 (NIV)

As a charity, BRF Ministries is always doing a huge assortment of things, from our **Anna Chaplaincy** team equipping people to minister to older people to our **Messy Church** team bringing Jesus to families across the world. From our **Parenting for Faith** ministry reaching parents and church leaders to transform ideas about how to raise God-connected children to our **Living Faith** resources, which span so many different topics to help people to develop their faith journey.

At a glance these activities might seem distant or disparate, but a closer look shows the vine from which all our ministries grow – the mission set out by Leslie Mannering over 100 years ago, to which we still hold today: inspiring people of all ages to grow in Christian faith. God is at the heart of all that we do, and we are hugely thankful for all the fruit we have born through these works over the last century and more.

We want to keep building on this work, adapting, growing and finding even more glorious ways for people to grow in their faith while still remaining rooted to our mission.

This work would not be possible without kind donations from individuals, charitable trusts and gifts in wills. If you would like to support us now and in the future, you can become a Friend of BRF Ministries by making a monthly gift of £2 or more. We thank you for your friendship.

Judith Moore
Fundraising development officer

| Give. Pray. Get involved. |
| **brf.org.uk** |

Please note our new subscription rates, current until 30 April 2025:

Individual subscriptions
covering 3 issues for under 5 copies, payable in advance
(including postage & packing):

	UK	Europe	Rest of world
New Daylight	£19.50	£26.85	£30.75
New Daylight 3-year subscription (9 issues) (not available for Deluxe)	£57.60	N/A	N/A
New Daylight Deluxe per set of 3 issues p.a.	£24.75	£33.15	£39.15

Group subscriptions
covering 3 issues for 5 copies or more, sent to one UK address (post free):

New Daylight	£14.97 per set of 3 issues p.a.
New Daylight Deluxe	£19.05 per set of 3 issues p.a.

Please note that the annual billing period for group subscriptions runs from 1 May to 30 April.

Overseas group subscription rates
Available on request. Please email **enquiries@brf.org.uk**.

Copies may also be obtained from Christian bookshops:

New Daylight	£4.99 per copy
New Daylight Deluxe	£6.35 per copy

> All our Bible reading notes can be ordered online
> by visiting **brfonline.org.uk/subscriptions**

NEW DAYLIGHT INDIVIDUAL SUBSCRIPTION FORM

All our Bible reading notes can be ordered online by visiting
brfonline.org.uk/subscriptions

Title _____ First name/initials _____ Surname _____

Address _____

_____ Postcode _____

Telephone _____ Email _____

Please send *New Daylight* beginning with the September 2024 / January 2025 / May 2025 issue (*delete as appropriate*):

(*please tick box*)	UK	Europe	Rest of world
New Daylight 1-year subscription	☐ £19.50	☐ £26.85	☐ £30.75
New Daylight 3-year subscription	☐ £57.60	N/A	N/A
New Daylight Deluxe	☐ £24.75	☐ £33.15	☐ £39.15

Optional donation to support the work of BRF Ministries £ _____

Total enclosed £ _____ (cheques should be made payable to 'BRF')

Please complete and return the Gift Aid declaration on page 141 to make your donation even more valuable to us.

Please charge my MasterCard / Visa with £ _____

Card no. | | | | | | | | | | | | | | | | |

Expires end | | | | | | Security code | | | | Last 3 digits on the reverse of the card

To set up a Direct Debit, please complete the Direct Debit instruction on page 159.

We will use your personal data to process this order. From time to time we may send you information about the work of BRF Ministries. Please contact us if you wish to discuss your mailing preferences. Our privacy policy is available at **brf.org.uk/privacy**.

Please return this form with the appropriate payment to:
BRF Ministries, 15 The Chambers, Vineyard, Abingdon OX14 3FE
For terms and cancellation information, please visit **brfonline.org.uk/terms**.

Bible Reading Fellowship is a charity (233280) and company limited by guarantee (301324), registered in England and Wales

ND0224

NEW DAYLIGHT GIFT SUBSCRIPTION FORM

☐ I would like to give a gift subscription (please provide both names and addresses):

Title _____ First name/initials _____ Surname _____

Address _____

_____ Postcode _____

Telephone _____ Email _____

Gift subscription name _____

Gift subscription address _____

_____ Postcode _____

Gift message (20 words max. or include your own gift card):

_____

_____

Please send *New Daylight* beginning with the September 2024 / January 2025 / May 2025 issue (*delete as appropriate*):

(*please tick box*)	UK	Europe	Rest of world
New Daylight 1-year subscription	☐ £19.50	☐ £26.85	☐ £30.75
New Daylight 3-year subscription	☐ £57.60	N/A	N/A
New Daylight Deluxe	☐ £24.75	☐ £33.15	☐ £39.15

Optional donation to support the work of BRF Ministries £ _____

Total enclosed £ _____ (cheques should be made payable to 'BRF')

Please complete and return the Gift Aid declaration on page 141 to make your donation even more valuable to us.

Please charge my MasterCard / Visa with £ _____

Card no. ☐☐☐☐ ☐☐☐☐ ☐☐☐☐ ☐☐☐☐

Expires end ☐☐ ☐☐ Security code ☐☐☐ Last 3 digits on the reverse of the card

To set up a Direct Debit, please complete the Direct Debit instruction on page 159.

We will use your personal data to process this order. From time to time we may send you information about the work of BRF Ministries. Please contact us if you wish to discuss your mailing preferences. Our privacy policy is available at **brf.org.uk/privacy**.

Please return this form with the appropriate payment to:
BRF Ministries, 15 The Chambers, Vineyard, Abingdon OX14 3FE
For terms and cancellation information, please visit **brfonline.org.uk/terms**.

Bible Reading Fellowship is a charity (233280) and company limited by guarantee (301324), registered in England and Wales

You can pay for your annual subscription to our Bible reading notes using Direct Debit. You need only give your bank details once, and the payment is made automatically every year until you cancel it. If you would like to pay by Direct Debit, please use the form opposite, entering your BRF account number under 'Reference number'.

You are fully covered by the Direct Debit Guarantee:

The Direct Debit Guarantee

- This Guarantee is offered by all banks and building societies that accept instructions to pay Direct Debits.

- If there are any changes to the amount, date or frequency of your Direct Debit, Bible Reading Fellowship will notify you 10 working days in advance of your account being debited or as otherwise agreed. If you request Bible Reading Fellowship to collect a payment, confirmation of the amount and date will be given to you at the time of the request.

- If an error is made in the payment of your Direct Debit, by Bible Reading Fellowship or your bank or building society, you are entitled to a full and immediate refund of the amount paid from your bank or building society.

- If you receive a refund you are not entitled to, you must pay it back when Bible Reading Fellowship asks you to.

- You can cancel a Direct Debit at any time by simply contacting your bank or building society. Written confirmation may be required. Please also notify us.

Instruction to your bank or building society to pay by Direct Debit

Please fill in the whole form using a ballpoint pen and return with order form to:

BRF Ministries, 15 The Chambers, Vineyard, Abingdon OX14 3FE

Service User Number: | 5 | 5 | 8 | 2 | 2 | 9 |

Name and full postal address of your bank or building society

To: The Manager	Bank/Building Society
Address	
	Postcode

Name(s) of account holder(s)

Branch sort code

☐ ☐ – ☐ ☐ – ☐ ☐

Bank/Building Society account number

☐ ☐ ☐ ☐ ☐ ☐ ☐ ☐

Reference number

☐ ☐ ☐ ☐ ☐ ☐ ☐ ☐

Instruction to your Bank/Building Society

Please pay Bible Reading Fellowship Direct Debits from the account detailed in this instruction, subject to the safeguards assured by the Direct Debit Guarantee. I understand that this instruction may remain with Bible Reading Fellowship and, if so, details will be passed electronically to my bank/ building society.

Signature(s)

Banks and Building Societies may not accept Direct Debit instructions for some types of account.

BRF Ministries

Inspiring people of all ages to grow in Christian faith

BRF Ministries is the
home of Anna Chaplaincy,
Living Faith, Messy Church
and Parenting for Faith

As a charity, our work would not be possible without
fundraising and gifts in wills.
To find out more and to donate,
visit brf.org.uk/give or call +44 (0)1235 462305